UNLEARNING RACISM
DIGGING UP OUR ROOTS

AMERICAN
SANKOFA

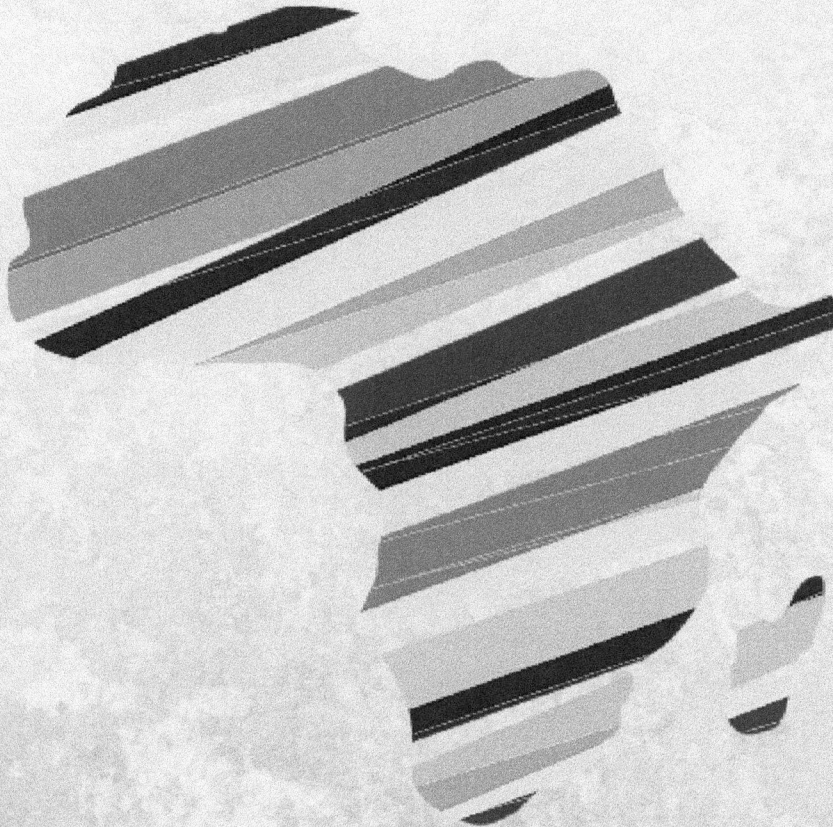

A Brief Introduction to American Racism
& African Civilization Before Slavery

Adrienne Smith

American Sankofa

Adrienne Smith

Copyright ©
First Edition July 2020
ISBN: 978-1-7353616-2-8
Library of Congress Control Number: 2020913528

Los Angeles, CA USA

www.bronzedmoon.com

www.bronzedmoon.com

©

For my Ancestors.

Thank you for leaving a light so bright

that it could not be buried.

Thank you for your guidance.

Thank you for surviving.

American Sankofa
Unlearning Racism
Digging up our Roots

Table of Contents:

Introduction:

This brief American Sankofa reflects on segments of my Black experience; pieces of African history that have remained with me. Pieces that have impacted me. The intensity in which living as a Black person in America has forced my eyes open, while simultaneously attempting to glue them shut. This is a collection of research sourced from scholars and intellectuals I've studied and admired for their preservation of history, and analysis of social dynamics affecting Black America. My goal is to share their words with you in a raw, digestible manuscript that echoes and magnifies their intent of sharing knowledge. This is all with the hope that each reader may be inspired to continue educating themselves around the Black American plight, victory, and connection to African greatness. Moreover, this affects the world. The African descendant has had an enormous impact on not only America, but several nations throughout history.

Individuals of varied backgrounds are exploring this topic for the first time, which is incredible. If you identify as Caucasian or white, it's important to recognize you've been taught history through a Eurocentric lens- we all have. This provides an automated entitlement, living with the perception that history is in fact 'yours'. In order for you to fully respect and advocate for the Black community, it's imperative you understand our truth in history. Everyone should be taught to fully appreciate the significant pieces that we, as Black people have contributed, and the intricacies that have made us who we are today. An ally, in this instance, references someone who is dedicated to fighting for social justice and against oppression although it may not affect them directly. The greatest allies are able to stand in their own discomfort, overcome prejudices, while listening to disenfranchised or underrepresented people. Subsequently, it's about taking action; walking alongside them; demanding change with genuine intention. Please, take a moment. Really- have a moment; take a deep breath. Be open to learning, and to letting your ego and preconceived notions go. This is meant to educate you so that you may retain the tools to form more complete, balanced opinions. Hold on to the idea that empathy and decency go a long way. Continue to combat and educate those who may be expressing false grievances when topics such as Black lives and livelihoods arise. Until we're all free, none of us are truly free. The equivalent applies to non-Black, POC (people of color.) We are all familiar with some level of struggle. There has been a realization that Black American resistance was not solely for our own civil rights, but extended reformation to immigration rights, native rights, and human rights here in America. Thank you for standing with us now; continuing to combat anti-blackness that exists not just within this country, but within your own cultures and communities as well. Pushing to unify and enlighten is truly a necessity.

Ultimately, to my Black American audience, who I'm reflecting with most inherently, we must realize the same. We must begin to view ourselves in the highest regard; remembering our magic- even when the world does not. Within this movement towards equality we each have a role to play; even if it's simply educating. One who knows them self, knows where they're going. It's time to know yourself, while making your history visible and sacred. This is liberating; and liberation is a form of magic. Energy is liberated when we break through status quo- rules that you were conditioned to believe, no longer apply. This energy strengthens the spirit.

"I speak not for myself but for those without voice... those who have fought for their rights... their right to live in peace, their right to be treated with dignity, their right to equality of opportunity, their right to be educated." -Malala Yousafzai

Sankofa is an African term, loosely translated as returning to the past to move forward or moving forward while looking back. It's symbolized as a stylized heart or a bird, with its neck facing backwards. Let's take a look back, with a resolve of gaining a better understanding of who Black Americans are, and where our African roots are buried. The intent is to conjure an 'American Sankofa.'

We'll place a fraction of our focus on unlearning white supremacy, while filling the gaps in history with its missing fragments collected in Africa. Let's all unlearn. White supremacy is simply an invention- a tool. At its very basic level it stands as a mouthpiece for hate, jealousy, & this false sense of comfort. Even deeper, it's been used traditionally as a veil by European invaders to assuage their own guilt as they'd invade countries, commit genocide, and build capitalistic systems on the backs of darker skinned people- all based on the idea that these people are lesser than. Racism is the base. Capitalism & classism stand on top of it comfortably.

Andre 3000 wore a shirt that begged the question:
"Across Cultures, darker people suffer most. Why?"
The Answer is summarized above.

The first step in reforming your own mind is accepting that you've been taught an incomplete, and very much skewed version of world history. Taking steps to uncover the impact African people have had on nearly every major segment of our shared history will help transform and strengthen the perception of who Black Americans are.

I'd encourage you to utilize elements in this piece as stepping stones, allow yourself to dig deeper into history and societal inequities. Employ use of search engines, libraries, the books and articles in the sources below. Have deeper conversations with your Black friends to continue unraveling the misinformation you may still be holding on to. Black readers, listen to yourselves and allow your own resilience to continue to uplift you. American Sankofa is meant to be a brief, concise, resource to guide you through thoughts and conversations around the inherent bias facing Black Americans.

PART 1:
"THAT'S NOT A CHIP ON MY SHOULDER. THAT'S YOUR FOOT ON MY NECK."

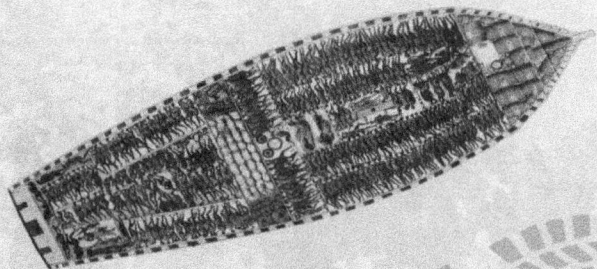

*Image: People on slave ship

"That's not a chip on my shoulder. That's your foot on my neck." -Malcolm X

America has had its foot on our necks since inception.

To those learning & continuing to be allies for the equality of Black people in America, let's remember this is a time to listen, practice empathy, and be *anti*-racist. White privilege is not always intentional, but at some level you are benefiting from it. James Baldwin describes America as a "complex country which insists on being very narrow minded." This is due in part to the invention of white supremacy & the comfort and power it allots. We'll further dissect how this has been so deeply ingrained into nearly every structure, & institution in America. Apathy is dangerous- you can no longer wade comfortably in the middle.

Overt White Supremacy
(Socially Unacceptable) Lynching
Hate Crimes
Blackface The N-word
Swastikas Neo-Nazis Burning Crosses
Racist Jokes Racial Slurs KKK

Calling the Police on Black People White Silence Colorblindness
White Parents Self-Segregating Neighborhoods & Schools **Covert White**
Eurocentric Curriculum White Savior Complex Spiritual Bypassing **Supremacy**
Education Funding from Property Taxes Discriminatory Lending **(Socially**
Mass Incarceration Respectability Politics Tone Policing **Acceptable)**
Racist Mascots Not Believing Experiences of BIPOC Paternalism
"Make America Great Again" Blaming the Victim Hiring Discrimination
"You don't sound Black" "Don't Blame Me, I Never Owned Slaves" Bootstrap Theory
School-to-Prison Pipeline Police Murdering BIPOC Virtuous Victim Narrative
Higher Infant & Maternal Mortality Rate for BIPOC "But What About Me?" "All Lives Matter"
BIPOC as Halloween Costumes Racial Profiling Denial of White Privilege
Prioritizing White Voices as Experts Treating Kids of Color as Adults Inequitable Healthcare
Assuming Good Intentions Are Enough Not Challenging Racist Jokes Cultural Appropriation
Eurocentric Beauty Standards Anti-Immigration Policies Considering AAVE "Uneducated"
Denial of Racism Tokenism English-Only Initiatives Self-Appointed White Ally
Exceptionalism Fearing People of Color Police Brutality Fetishizing BIPOC Meritocracy Myth
"You're So Articulate" Celebration of Columbus Day Claiming Reverse-Racism Paternalism
Weaponized Whiteness Expecting BIPOC to Teach White People Believing We Are "Post-Racial"
"But We're All One Big Human Family" / "There's Only One Human Race" Housing Discrimination

Source: @thecönciöuskid

Learning to be "Anti-racist," means identifying (the above) more covert faces of racism-

calling them out and helping to dismantle them. One note regarding racism- especially

racism here in America- it's not always loud, overt and tacky.

Allies in the movement:

So glad you've found your voice.

Keep allowing your empathy & humanity to lead.

Don't question yourself for speaking up.

The only people you're offending are racists.

Let them see themselves- they don't have space to hide.

Call them out.

Educate.

Magnify.

Racists are defensive.

Whether it's conscious or not.

They gaslight.

Deny.

Deflect.

Victimize themselves.

Divide, & call you divisive.

This idea of whiteness has somehow convinced them that it provides a greater standing.

It's just that- an idea.

It's an idea that they hold on to for comfort.

It's time for a shift.

As most of Black *American* history begins with slavery, Black history does not. Let's address slavery first. Although we'll start here, we undoubtedly will not conclude here. Slavery is a piece of American history that must not be overlooked, or diminished- but also needs to be expanded upon and derived from to maintain the full story of who Black Americans are. Slavery is the root that grew the tree which is America. It is the base that holds its foundation. Slavery ripped African people from their native lands- robbed their dignity. People who were already established parents, doctors, farmers, laborers; carpenters, astronomers, spiritual leaders, men & women with a history- full, thriving lives before they were wrenched away. Whippings. Beatings. Rape. Permanent metal bars on necks to prevent comfortable sleep or living. The removal of limbs. Separation from offspring. Rape of both women, and men. Being gaslit into submission- often through skewed Christian teachings; with the first slave ship being named Jesus. Again, not solely to pacify the slaves, but to provide the slave owners and the apathetic white population some false validation that it was acceptable. American Chattel slavery presented a new low in history- completely based on skin color, negating the opportunity to escape, and more terrorizing and inhumane than any level of former enslavement. Being stuffed- foot to head, body over body in the basement of the ships that crossed the Atlantic. Separated from family, culture and any life they'd known. Even recent claims of Irish slavery being equally damaging were refuted during Frederick Douglass' four month visit to Ireland. As a former slave himself, he concluded that "the

Irish, unlike slaves, had the freedom to marry, to protest, to move around and to emigrate. In contrast Negro-slavery consisted not in taking away a man's property, but in making property of him, and in destroying his identity—in treating him as the beasts and creeping things."

Slavery has had a profound economic impact on this country. The enslaved proved to be America's largest financial asset from 1801 to 1862; as the amount of cotton picked daily increased 400 percent. The profits from cotton propelled the US as a leading economy on the world stage. Slaves were used as collateral to develop banks, build companies, universities, & wealth for white American families. African slaves built the American world as we know it, yet descendants are withheld the equity, and mere respect they deserve. Nearly every historic structure, admired, or revered in this country was built by Black African slave labor. In construction of the U.S. Capital, three hundred and eighty-five payments were made to the owners of African American slaves. Still, no reparations for descendants of slaves. In 1833, Britain used £20 million, 40% of its national budget to buy freedom for its slaves. The money transferred directly to slave *owners*; completed by taxpayers only in the recent year of 2015. The estimated value of the enslaved population by 1860 reached over seven times the value of currency in circulation. Slavery has had such an unescapable impact on Black people that studies have shown engrained DNA trauma on its descendants today; generations removed.

Trauma- let's rest on this for a moment. Trauma is defined as 'a deep, emotional wound.' Most people carry some form of trauma- possibly stemming from childhood, or a distressing experience. Now, imagine hundreds of years of trauma carried on through descendants; disrupting emotions, cognitive reaction, even increasing health risks. Toxic stress- strong, frequent, or prolonged adversity affects your physical being. Epigenetics refer to how the experiences of previous generations will affect who we are. Post Traumatic Slave Syndrome is a condition that exists as a consequence of centuries of chattel slavery followed by institutionalized racism and oppression. It has resulted in multigenerational adaptive behavior; few positive attributes such as resilience, with the majority being harmful and detrimental. It's most important to seek healing. Address this trauma in order to recover and develop the ability to live fully. America must also amend the trauma imposed upon its Black citizens by evaluating the continued internal bias & privilege it exhibits, along with a thorough examination of its external societal structures and systems.

There were assorted myths placed into circulation with a goal of justifying the slave trade. We'll touch on this as we go deeper into American history, African history, and the history of Europeans colonizing Africa. The largest simply proclaiming that Europeans came to Africa to spread civilization. This is entirely false in premise, as Africa was ancient upon arrival. Rich in resources, with well-designed cities, and highly developed people. According to documentation from explorers, its inhabitants were "civilized to the marrow of his bones." To justify the destruction of an already organized, well-functioning, and sufficient people, the monster that still haunts our lives today originated. This monster is racism. [1]

Link Here to Youtube Video on The Slave Trade

---

[1] **Trigger warning: Disturbing Images on next page

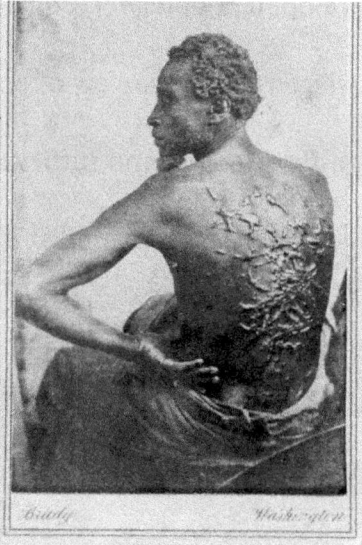

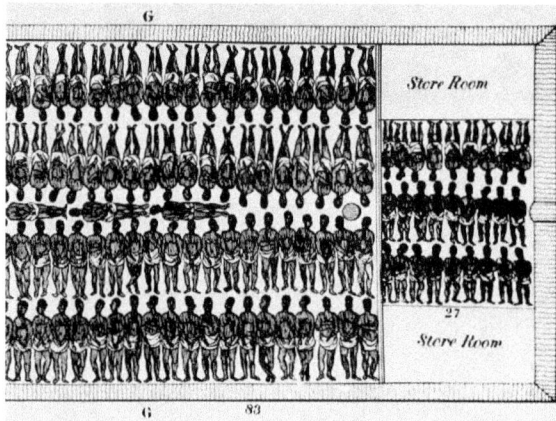

In a recent conversation with my paternal Grandmother, born & raised in a small

southern town, she recalled memories from the beginning of her 90 years. Memories of

her grandmother- a former slave. Her mannerisms, even trivial traditions like sweeping her yard with a broom- not keeping grass in it for some reason; these rituals stemming from slavery. I offer this simply for perspective; we're not so far removed from these centuries of enslavement we reference. America is still near the beginning of true freedom for its Black citizens.

These are a few of my recent ancestors- great, great grandparents- direct descendants of slaves.

Expressed best by Ralph Wiley, "Give me the free labor of one Black person for a year, I would be a rich man. Give me the free labor of a dozen Black people for one year, I would be a very rich man. Give me the free labor of millions of Black people for 250 years, I would be America." We could craft an entirely separate dissertation on the mass effects of slavery, outlining the case for an estimate of what's owed of upwards of $24 Trillion in reparations.

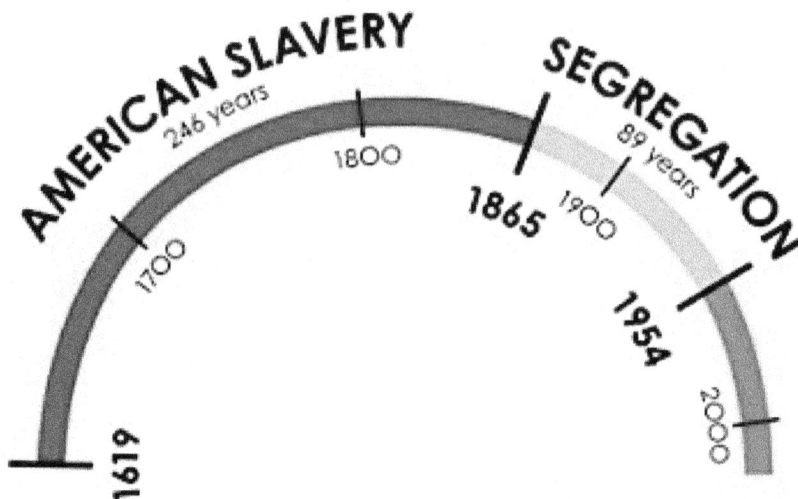

AMERICAN SLAVERY
246 years
1700
1800
SEGREGATION
89 years
1865
1900
1954
2000
1619

My own mother grew up traveling the South with the 'Green Book' when her family vacationed. It offered assistance & direction for safe hotels/safe spaces for Black families; resorting to sleeping in their car when unavailable. She was one of the first to integrate schools in her hometown. My father remembers sundown towns, which prohibited Black citizens from living; mandating they vacate by sunset- often signaled by bells or horns. This is one generation removed.

In Frederick Douglass' infamous speech, 'What to the slave is the Fourth of July,' he expressed it clearly: "I say it with a sad sense of the disparity between us. I am not included within the pale of glorious anniversary! Your high independence only reveals the immeasurable distance between us... The rich inheritance of justice, liberty, prosperity and independence, bequeathed by your fathers is shared by you, not by me. The sunlight that brought light and healing to you, has brought stripes and death to me."

Although I've been privileged to be raised in a middle class, military household, the disparities have not eluded me- we're still building family wealth, from scratch. Currently, white families hold a 10x advantage in the wealth gap. Overwhelmingly, Black businesses are denied or offered smaller loans. We are habitually not allotted 'gift' money for down payments on homes, or college tuition simply because it doesn't exist. Instead of having any form of wealth passed down, the younger generations are striving to build it for themselves- simultaneously helping sustain the older generation of parents & grandparents.

Every aspect of government, religion, private and public enterprise was craftly employed to cripple Black prospects for success after slavery. The issue today is that not much of this has been reformed or fully overturned. It's 2020 & we're still fighting for equality in education, loan access, food access, real estate; reform in policing, government, disparities in imprisonment, among simply being deserved to be treated as decent citizens. We're going on seven years of Flint, Michigan lacking access to clean water. Today, I learned that in the report on Breonna Taylor's death- being slaughtered in her sleep, shot eight times by officers who'd performed a 'no-knock' raid on her home- it was confirmed that her injuries were "none." Today, I signed a petition to change the status of the KKK to a Domestic Terrorism organization; just today. Why must we beg America to simply do right? Possibly, because America does not inherently include us. Many are recognizing that we may not separate this country's proclaimed status as the greatest nation in the world from one with the most extensive relationships with human bondage.

Images: Sanitation workers strike in Memphis 1968. Below: Birmingham demonstrations 1963, MLK being arrested

Smithsonian, Library of Congress

"White people's belief in the fairness of America is a fantasy of self-deception and comfortable vanity." -Martin Luther King Jr.

PART 2:

AS A **DIRECT RESULT** OF SLAVERY

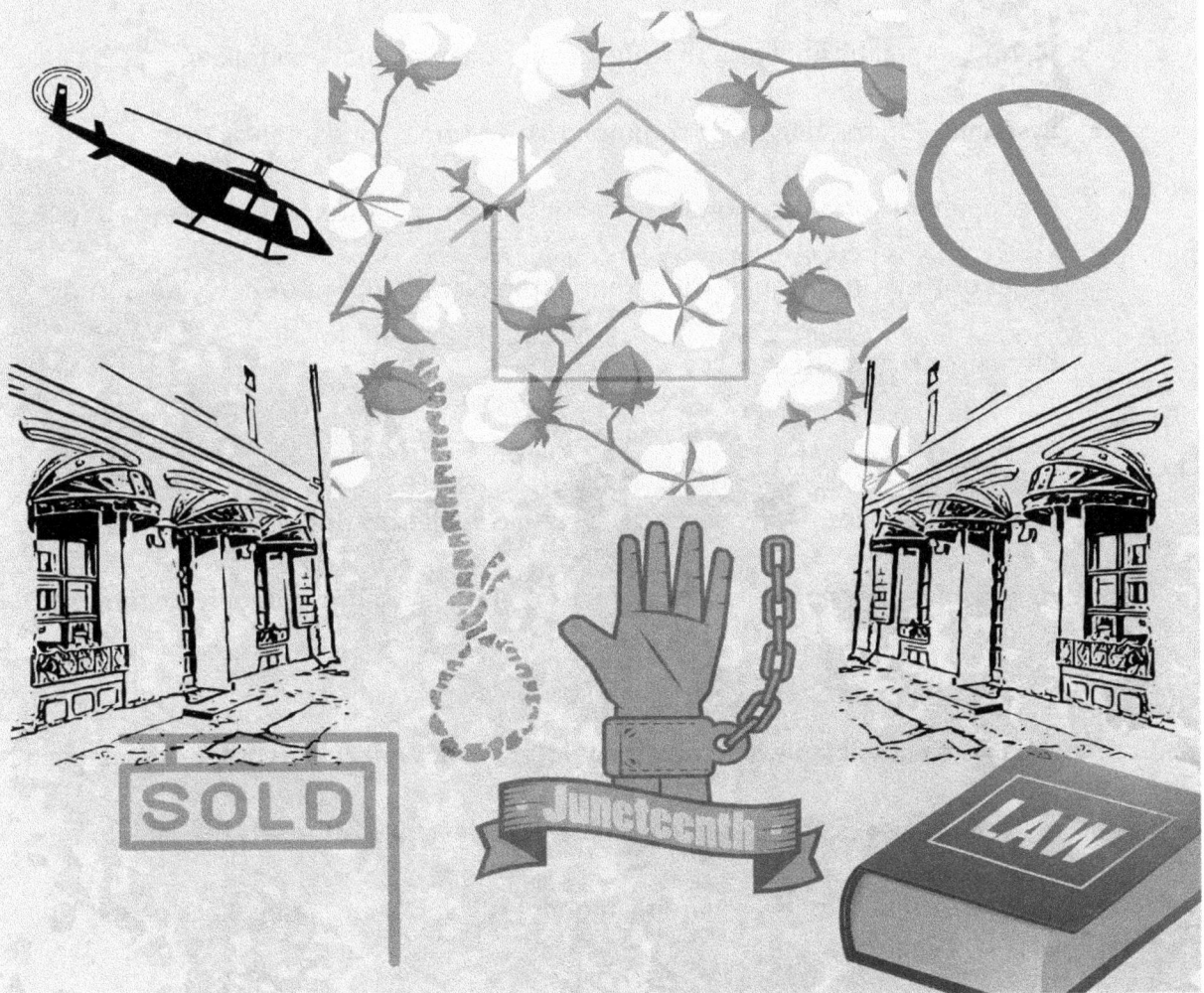

As a Direct Result of Slavery:

Traditionally, Black people in America were not considered fully human- only a fraction. Upon Emancipation, not a single of the promised and deserved resolutions were distributed. No "40 acres," no "mule." The idea that a country formed with a solid unwavering base of slavery would provide any form of true equity is dubious.

- Systematic- "relating to or consisting of a system... "methodical in procedure or plan." Systematic implies a thorough series of steps that you follow.
- Systemic- "of, relating to, or common to a system... fundamental to a predominant social, economic, or political practice. Systemic is not related to a series of steps. It is a quality inherent in the system, not necessarily on purpose, but more "that's just the way it works."

Where systematic applies to an approach, systemic applies to the system itself. Regarding racism, either apply. American racism is both systemic & deeply systematic.

Examining an American staple like the original New York Wall Street; other than being a literal wall built by slaves, it originated as a bustling slave market itself. The direct connection that remains today, regarding money- still vastly excluding Black people holds great irony. America as a country, must acknowledge that millions of enslaved Black Americans were the 'boots' as well as the 'strap' of our economic system. As you may be aware, directly after slavery Black people worked together, building communities up in separate, thriving towns- sometimes called *Black* Wall Street. The location in Tulsa, we're most familiar with, was burned to the ground- in a jealousy fueled, government sanctioned, white-mob rage; leaving hundreds of corpses in its wake. Others, like the Black Wall Street in Durham, NC were ravaged and torn apart with programs like 'urban renewal.'

There is **another massacre** that stands out- this one in Elaine, Ark, also occurring in the summer of 1919, known as 'Red Summer' due to the numerous Black murders committed via hanging, burning, or slaughter. A group of African American citizens gathered in a church, meeting to discuss fair farming. Authorities deemed it an insurrection and shot into the church. That's it- that's all it took was for someone to feel threatened by the potential of Black success and be automatically defended, even backed up with their right to react. Black officials shot back. Below you'll find short clip of what followed, as hundreds were eventually slaughtered with the authorization of authorities: "The following morning, Gov. Charles H. Brough of Arkansas and a World War I veteran, Col. Issac Jencks escorted 583 soldiers, including a machine gun battalion, from Camp Pike in Little Rock, the state capital, to Elaine. Colonel Jencks sent all of the white women and children to Helena by train, ordered the immediate disarming of everyone and authorized the killing of Black insurgents who failed to disarm. Then the real massacre began: For the next five days, Colonel Jencks and his troops, assisted by vigilantes, hunted Black people over a 200-mile radius. They scorched and burned homes with families inside, slaughtered and tortured others. The troops were aided by seven machine guns. On Oct. 7, Colonel Jencks declared the insurrection over and withdrew his troops. He brought the men and women deemed insurrectionists to the Phillips County jail in Helena. On Oct. 31, a grand jury indicted 122 Black men and women for offenses ranging from murder to night riding. A jury convicted 12 Black men in the murders of three white men, even though two of the deaths had occurred from white people accidentally shooting each other in a frenzy. The "confessions" of the Black men had been secured through torture. Black people were thus blamed, sentenced and jailed for their own massacre." [2]

---

[2] **Trigger warning: Disturbing image on next page

Mass Lynching

After slavery, "Black people held a virtual monopoly of almost all skilled and unskilled labor. Blacks were without a rival... & had 95% of all the industrial work in the southern states." -Thomas Nelson Page

- The first **Affirmative Action** programs were set up for whites- seeking advantages for them, as they began competing against the same former slaves whose talents were once the "major breadwinners" for *their* families.

- Somehow, as affirmative action has shifted to offer equality for underrepresented groups, certain people felt threatened over equality & have perpetuated the myth that it promotes 'reverse racism.'

- Jumping to modern manifestations of these notions, I've been told that I've gotten a job because I was filling a slot as a Black woman, with affirmative action. This is demeaning and ignores the fact that there should be space for us regardless- it should actually be pushed for. I've now chosen to divest myself from things that don't serve me- especially jobs. I've been told bluntly I'm the only Black person someone has met- imagine the burden of speaking for millions of unique individual people. (We will get into these forms of microaggressions shortly.) This story is duplicated all over corporate America.

- Unions were originally created to remove Blacks from these jobs and industries they dominated; due to the skills crafted and perfected during slavery. The jobs were passed along to European immigrants who were flooding in by the millions. This locked the Black man into the lowest-wage labor, or even completely jobless.

- Black workers have always stood out as innovative and highly skilled. Contributing to some of the biggest inventions of the Industrial revolution and on- the rotary blade that improved the lawn mower (John Albert Burr), modern elevator (Alexander Miles), refrigerator (Frederick McKinley Jones), even Thomas Edison's family empire is "based almost entirely on the genius of a Black man." (Lewis Latimer)

- Currently, as we examine several of the confederate statues being pulled down, rather than continuing to debate with people grasping to hold high the ugliest parts of history, let's excavate statues in the honor of forgotten Black American legends. As the debate over 'heritage,' or potentially erasing history prevails, let's consider that some people don't need reminders of the racist American traitors who terrorized their family for decades. It has persisted throughout generations- leaving some Black Americans affected with a constant visible reminder: "I have rape-colored skin. My light-brown-blackness is a living testament to the rules, the practices, the causes of the Old South. If there are those who want to remember the legacy of the Confederacy, if they want monuments, well, then, my body is a monument. My skin is a monument."

-Poetry by Caroline Randall Williams

Real Estate/Land

How does a system built on white supremacy in turn foster a severe lack of opportunity for those that are not white; especially Black Americans?

- The Homestead Act (1862) gave up 160 free acres for white families only- 1.6M families approximately- this was approximately 10% of land in the U.S; keeping in mind this was still stolen land from the Natives.

- Some of this land was sold to corporations, cultivated farms, while many still had Black families sharecropping on the land (as my grandfather did.) Regardless, these families built their land gifts into family estates- building a solid source of wealth.

- Other government sanctioned land grab programs that benefited whites only & affected up to 35 million white families included the Preemption Act (1830), & The Mineral Leasing Act (1920)

- Well into the 20th century, banks implemented 'red-lining'- coded racism. Policies where FHA decision makers literally sat around & drew red lines around Black neighborhoods on a map refusing mortgages, home insurance, financing, and loans to everyone inside of those boundaries. This continued through the 60s. When Blacks were finally allowed mortgages, they were often of lesser value, and predatory. This should be strongly considered when we examine a transfer of family wealth- not having access to build that wealth in the first place.

- An example of the types of mortgages that were given to Black people include stories like one from a man named Clyde Ross, highlighted in Ta Nehisi Coates "A Case for Reparations" who moved to Chicago for opportunity, as well as some kind of protection under the law. He'd bought "on contract": a predatory agreement that combined all the responsibilities of homeownership with all the disadvantages of renting—while offering the benefits of neither. Ross had bought his house for $27,500. The seller, not the previous homeowner but a new kind of middleman, had bought it for only $12,000 six months before selling it to Ross. In a contract sale, the seller kept the deed until the contract was paid in full—and, unlike with a normal mortgage, Ross would acquire no equity in the meantime. If he missed a single payment, he would immediately forfeit his $1,000 down payment, all his monthly payments, and the property itself."

- Consider this, especially before gentrifying a traditionally African American neighborhood- assess what it may have taken for this neighborhood to get to where it is, where these people will go when they are displaced.

- Black Billionaire Robert Smith offers a bold solution for new opportunity and funding for Black businesses through the largest banks in his "2% Solution." A bold plan to funnel billions into Black businesses. The same banks that were built off of our exploitation, and our literal bodies as collateral may offer opportunities- it's not equality that we need, it's equity.

- With Black banks today, access to capital, which is needed to help build and uplift communities is lacking most. Just recently, Netflix has deposited $100 Million into Black owned banks. Other companies leading equity and change should join in not just diversifying dollars spent, but who they hire, and support.

- **Jim Crow** was established not plainly to demean Black Americans with separate and unequal bathrooms/water fountains, or entrances, but to hinder Black people from accumulating property, starting businesses, engaging in trade and commerce, and especially establishing an economic base independent of white people.

- Additional Jim Crow laws that eliminated Blacks businesses as economic competitors include the denial of bank loans, refusing white wholesalers to supply Black businesses, denial of education for Black citizens, discriminatory real estate practices, police repression, lack of access to the political arena, added with local massacres & terrorism.

- Lynching and racial terror were used as a tool to enforce Jim Crow laws. The tradition of terrorizing the entire local Black community, vs. just one suspected offender also instilled a deep fear.

- There were incidents of Black people being attacked for minor infractions including not removing their hats or refusing to hand over a whiskey flask. African Americans were frequently lynched for non-criminal violations including speaking to white people with less respect or than believed was due.

- Parents and spouses sent loved ones away who'd suddenly found themselves at risk of being lynched for a minor social transgression. Frantic, desperate escapes, surviving near-lynching eventually led to many fleeing the south altogether.

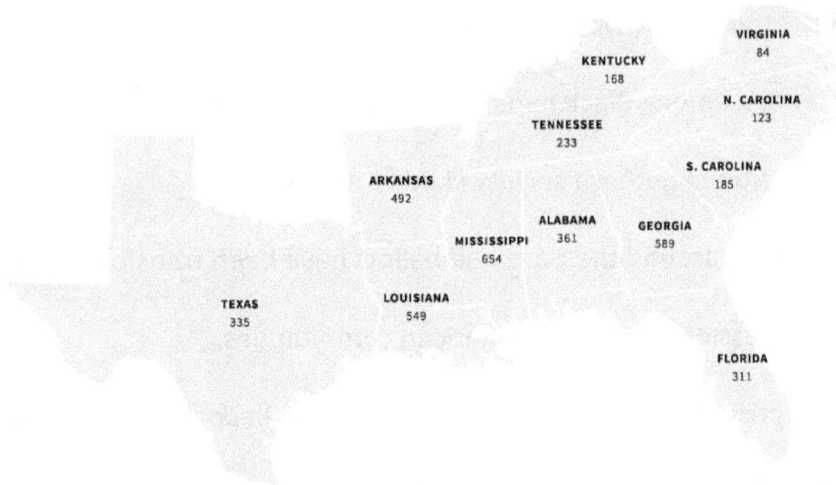

VIRGINIA
84

KENTUCKY
168

N. CAROLINA
123

TENNESSEE
233

S. CAROLINA
185

ARKANSAS
492

ALABAMA
361

GEORGIA
589

MISSISSIPPI
654

TEXAS
335

LOUISIANA
549

FLORIDA
311

Lynching stats 1877-1950 https://lynchinginamerica.eji.org/report/

- "Through lynching, Southern white communities asserted their racial dominance over the region's political and economic resources—a dominance first achieved through slavery would now be restored through blood and terror."

- In certain parts of the south, to be employed anywhere other than a plantation (doing sharecropping work,) Black workers needed a license granted by a judge, while it was required the employer be white. If they left for any reason it meant they could be arrested and placed on a public works project which included clearing forests, draining swamps, building roads, bridges, railroads, and canals. Many of these traditions, deeply sinking into America's Prison system. Take for example California's current statistic of its 40% nearly free-labor, prison-based firefighters, saving the state over $100 Million each year.

- Racial segregation often translated to the complete exclusion of Black people from institutions, and opportunities. This separation made way for a stark disadvantage among Black people and proved to be a consistent symbol of the inferior position Southern society liked to assert.

- Jim Crow laws around the polls and ballots have been transformed today into voter suppression for African American communities.

- Voter suppression has only continued into 2020; becoming even more insidious. During primaries in Kentucky, the 3500+ polling places were reduced to 200. In Jefferson County, KY with over 600,000 residents, half identifying as Black, there was just one location.

Personally, attending a Historically Black College- North Carolina A&T State University, provided an acute awareness of the need to study and ponder on the depths of our history. My African American Studies professor declared the class on day one:

"Everything you've been taught about history is a lie." I realized, even in this hyperbole, that even if it was not a lie- there was most likely an omission. This man held power in his voice; commanding power. He was a true educator at heart. I mention him because he changed my life, even after *his* life as he'd known it was taken away. My professor was a Black Panther- who was held as a political prisoner. It should be expressed- the goal of the original Black Panther organization was to defend, and help liberate the unprotected Black community, when the police and government did not, while offering deeper solutions for advancement. This was reimagined by the media & government agencies, as well as those who feared their strength. Whether staging lawful, arm-bearing silent protests with a fist in the air or developing community programs for Black mothers with children in need of food- this organizing held too much of a threat to traditional systems of oppression.

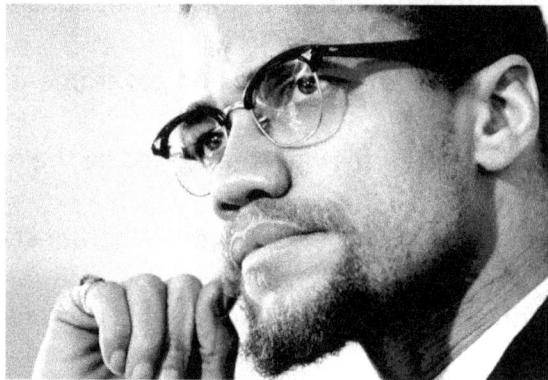

Several major leaders within the Black Panther organization have been assassinated.

Notably Fred Hampton, along with other Black leaders of civil movements- MLK, Medgar

Evers, and my own kin, Malcolm X. At every transition, every period of American history,

there has been a disproportionate level of targeted terror against Black people. Even in

2020, on the heels of the most mobilizing & change-bearing demonstration in the last

few decades, the reason for, and reaction to the Black Lives Matter movement proves

that this American terror has not ceased.

Sparked by the death of George Floyd, after a police officer kneeled intentionally on his neck for 8 minutes & 46 seconds; along with Breonna Taylor- shot 8 times in her sleep during a 'no knock raid.' Additionally, Elijah McClain- a severely gentle and introverted young man who 'played the piano for kittens,' choked, beaten & injected with ketamine on his walk home- later succumbing to death. The attention now comes as a wakeup call for empathy and action. This, after so many Americans were outraged over the silent, peaceful protest of NFL player Colin Kapernick, kneeling simply to acknowledge that everyone's 'America' is not a dream.

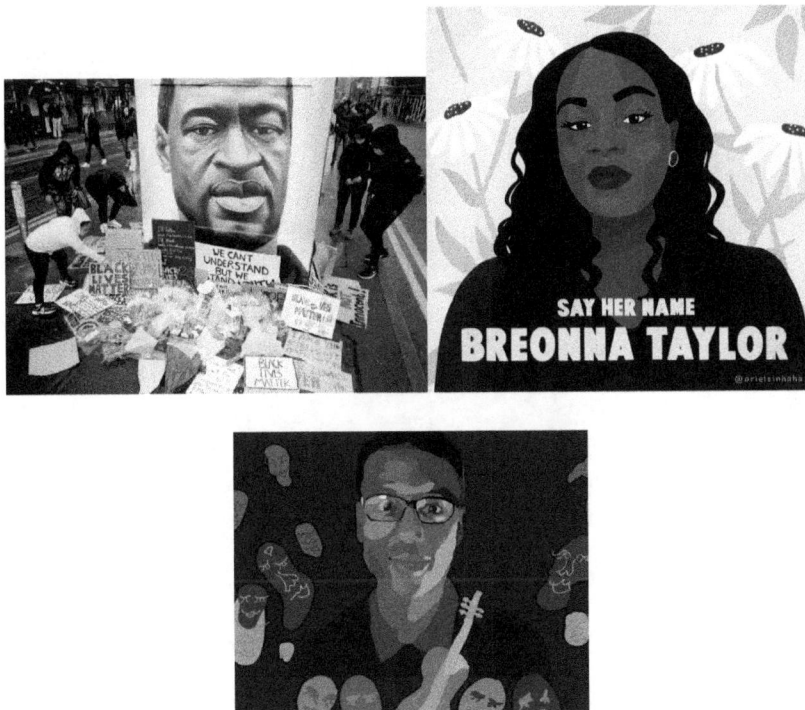

Photos: CNN, LA Times, artist Ariel Sinha, newsbreak, artist:

The outrage that segments of white America have expressed after simply being asked to address racial disparities in this country masks a deep insecurity of disturbing their comfort and exposing who this country truly is; what she holds in her depths. A fear of uncovering the guilt that's been veiled for years- covered by validation, excuses and denial. We're not here to debate the validity of a wrongful death, or the impact of a #Blacklivesmatter 'hashtag.' We are ushering in an awakening; a reckoning if you will, for those who've had the cowardly privilege of hiding behind racism for so long. For those who have unknowingly upheld and disregarded this issue for so long.

This is What the Black Lives Matter Movement looks like, 2020.

(Full Video on the magnitude: https://www.instagram.com/tv/CBHk3rkJj7V/)

Photos: Forbes, Vogue AU, France24
Washington DC, Los Angeles, Paris

The Best Way to dismantle systems built against you is by revealing to them who they are, in unity.

PART 3:

PRISON PIPELINE CLEAR IT OUT

"In our community it's too much policing & not enough justice." -Alex Long, Charm City

(PBS Documentary)

The U.S. makes up 5% of the world's population, yet 25% of the world's prison

population. For the most comprehensive breakdown of how the Prison system

disproportionately affects Black people, I'd suggest these as a starting point: "The New

Jim Crow" book, Documentary "13th," or movies "When they See Us," & "American

Violet." Or, sit down and have a conversation with your Black friends- even many of the

most successful Black people in America have not managed to escape either being

arrested, unprotected or terrorized by police. Stories of being pulled over for an air-

freshener on your rearview mirror 'obstructing view,' an unwarranted arrest for not

having the intel to share with cops where to find a gun, drugs planted on you then

having to fight & exhaust resources to regain your freedom, walking a new route to

school to avoid violent police harassment. Being a teenager, being roped to a tree by a

cop- after dark, left there for hours just to 'scare' you. Scaring, view-shifting,

experiences. These are individual experiences shared with me by Black men dear to me-

raised in a contrasting America; stories for another day.

Before we jump into stats on policing and America's prison system, let's resist the urge

to argue 'Black on Black crime.' Instead, ask yourself why some of these young Black men have been stalked with devastating crime from every angle; often stemming from broken family structures, desperate poverty, and trauma. Black people are not uniquely predisposed to commit crimes against each other; crime is generally racially segregated. Consider most white criminals- murders, rapes, shootings by white people, are usually committed upon other white people. We just don't call it 'white on white crime.' Black on Black crime was a term coined in the 80s- around the same time crack cocaine was admittedly funneled into Black neighborhoods, ripping apart households and contributing to the demise of once solid communities. Intensifying ghettos and impoverished people battling diminishing jobs, food deserts, disproportionate levels of education and opportunity; leaving them collectively dazed and partially stagnant. Not all Black people come from these spaces; regardless we're all working towards developing these communities with solutions & preventative measures to bring in further self-sufficiency. We view crime in our own communities to be just as important an issue as crime perpetrated against us. The crime we're referring to deals with the systemic policies, the manner in which we're mistreated, and the development of a new 'slavery,' within the American Prison Industrial Complex.

"Where justice is denied, where poverty is enforced, where ignorance prevails, and where any one class is made to feel that society is an organized conspiracy to oppress, rob and degrade them, neither persons nor property will be safe." -Frederick Douglass

- A "loophole" in the 13th Amendment permits re-enslavement through incarceration. That "exception" continued building America and does so today.

- When we say Prison "Pipeline" this means, especially starting from school-age, Black children are criminalized, and punished at harsher rates- leading to a pipeline into prisons.

- Being pulled out of class, even jailed without guardian knowledge, punished harsher for speaking out, being automatically excluded from higher level classes are all too frequent accounts of disparate treatment of Black students.

- Prison population from the time of "emancipation" has stayed consistent for white people but has risen up to 900% for Black Americans. This is largely due to targeted policing, lack of representation, forced plea deals, for-profit prison systems, arrest quotas, literal KKK-white supremist members masking as cops, etc...

- "14 Million whites vs. 2.6 Million Black people report using an illicit drug... yet for these same offenses, Blacks are sent to prison at 10x the rate of whites. & serve nearly as much time for drugs (58.7 months) as whites do for a violent offense. (61.7 months) (2014)

- As the 'The War on Drugs' ramped up, anti-drug funding increased exponentially, while funding for treatment withered away. Black people were largely shuffled away and imprisoned at alarmingly fast rates for nonviolent, often first-offense crimes.

- How does this compare to slavery? As a prisoner, you become the government's legal property leased to private companies for manual labor at nearly no cost, while enduring deplorable conditions; dehumanized with various levels of social and psychological control.

- Currently, the Federal government and 27 individual states utilize private prisons- this means the prison is not successful unless it is being filled. Simply, they are making money from taxpayers to imprison more people.

- Two of the largest **private prison companies**- Corrections Corporation of America and GEO Group showed over $3.3 Billion in Revenue in the early 2010s. Prisoners are contracted out to work for minimal wages like 23 cents an hour for companies including McDonalds, Boeing, Lockheed Martin, and several others There are tax credits given to businesses who've set up facilities inside of a prison, as well as "Prison Investment Bonds" that benefit companies like Allstate, American Express, and Merrill-Lynch.

- It's enormously cheaper to fund training, education, support and therapy programs- literally much cheaper to put these tax dollars toward education vs. prison systems which often never reform those who need it most.

- It costs more for New Jersey to pay for someone to go to prison then it does to go to Princeton. In California, the state spends over $48,000 on each prisoner, while just over $7,400 on students.

- Within certain states the cost is up to $67,000- again, directly from tax dollars.

- It should be noted that several banks and large companies also got their start through slavery- using Black American slaves as collateral for loans.

- The U.S. currently spends about $182 Billion locking people up each year

- Most people are so underrepresented and threatened with more time in jail that they'll result in plea-bargains. This means, they are unable to bring their cases to trial; and even if they're innocent they end up pleading guilty, to avoid a heftier sentence.

- "What's happening in Melody, TX is happening all around the country. Drug task forces use military tactics to terrorize people of color. Meanwhile, federal money goes to the counties that convict the most people and plea bargains are aggressively pushed to hasten those convictions." Texas law says you can be indicted off of the word of one informant- then they arrest you, make you take the plea, or else. - 'American Violet' (Movie, based on true events)

- 95% of people are in jail due to plea bargains.

- There are countless reformatory actions that need to be enforced: 'Stop and Frisk,' the Police departments policing themselves, immunity they're granted when they commit a crime, unwarranted searches, seizures, raids etc... The police force itself transformed into what it is today from literal slave patrols originating in the south. It's necessary to hold them accountable, have real training, and truly be overseen by the people they serve.

- A simple example: ensuring coroners have actual medical training (28 states don't require any formal medical training and 66% of deaths from police related injury were misclassified by coroners in 2015.)

- Officers have intentionally or unintentionally killed thousands of people- an estimate of over 6,000 (2013-2017) with less than 1.7% even being charged with a crime. People are simply asking for accountability.

Have you ever been stopped and frisked?

This is a regular occurrence for many young men and women,

overwhelmingly Black and brown

- Eight cities have police departments that kill Black men at a percentage higher than the national average murder rate. So, when it comes to comfortably living for example, in addition to searching for a home with the best schools, friendly neighbors, and amenities, Black families often must consider if they're living in a space that respects their life.

Police Spending Per Capita In Major U.S. Cities

Amount spent on policing per person in selected U.S. cities in 2020

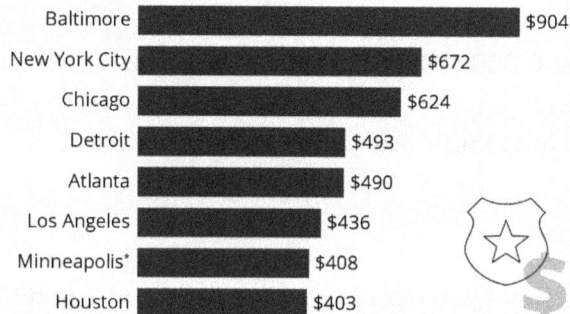

Baltimore	$904
New York City	$672
Chicago	$624
Detroit	$493
Atlanta	$490
Los Angeles	$436
Minneapolis*	$408
Houston	$403

* Latest Minneapolis data is from 2017
Source: The Center for Popular Democracy

statista

"Growing up here, you knew the ends and out of how to navigate around police. Police violence was normal. Learning to survive was necessary." -Black man from Baltimore, MD

Photo: Devin Allen, Time Magazine Cover

- Calls for police reform have echoed out for decades. The final report of the Obama Administration's 'President Task Force on 21st Century Policing,' resulted in some procedural tweaks. Even a member of the task force, Tracey Mears noted in 2017 "policing as we know it must be abolished before it can be transformed." People are asking for the billions that go into excessive programs such as militarizing the police or locking people up for cannabis should be reallocated to community programs, health, education, housing etc...

How Much Is The Police's Military Equipment Worth?

Value and quantity of selected military equipment transferred to law enforcement

	Value	Quantity
Mine resistant vehicle	$582.95m	849
Aircraft – fixed & rotary wing	$432.94m	458
Utiliy trucks	$284.98m	5,608
5.56 millimeter rifles	$27.83m	64,689
Combat/assault/ tactical wheeled vehicles	$21.90m	97
Armored trucks	$19.65m	302
Image intensifier, night vision	$19.45m	5,141
Communications equipment	$15.00m	3
Unmanned vehicles	$12.86m	72
Thermal sights	$12.36m	1,346

Total value of all former military property held by law enforcement agencies
$1,888,559,339

As of May 2018. Value based on DoD purchase price
Source: LESO via RAND

statista

- Police waste over $3B enforcing marijuana laws. While Black and white people use cannabis at an overall equal rate, depending on the state- Black people are 3.5-8.5x more likely to be arrested.

- Feds transfer about $7 Billion in war equipment to police departments which further militarizes them and enforces abuse of power.

- Just one of the egregious abuses of the Baltimore City police department include being caught in 2018 keeping fake guns available to plant on people they may happen to shoot.

- Watch a documentary on how people are living in these incredibly poverty-stricken cities- like the Charm City Documentary (by PBS on Amazon.) Baltimore is a city I mention often due to its stark, nearly third world conditions, and the roots I hold there. In certain areas, the unemployment rate is over 50%- the drug epidemic has completely ravaged the city; guns and murders are a public health crisis. People need help; the youth need direction. What's required is access, education, training, mentorship, therapy. They desperately need a police force that stems from the same neighborhoods; similar demographics, and less of a militarized, quota-driven method. Place this money into spaces that will in turn impact the community. Our communities need hope.

Photo: Devin Allen

This is why there's a conscious generation focused on defunding police departments.

This is what is meant when we express, 'defund the police.' Allocate less money here,

and more to spaces that bring about real change. A first step in a roster of change that

must follow.

PART 4:

MICROAGGRESSIONS & INEQUITIES

Microaggressions and Inequities:

We'll keep this succinct, as most people are now able to recognize and call out microaggressions. As an anti-racist, it's important to do so, in order for habits to change. Microaggressions are forms of jabs that are usually not so obvious- a bit more discrete. Defined as: "brief and commonplace daily verbal, behavioral, or environmental indignities, whether purposeful or not, communicate hostile, derogatory, or negative prejudicial slights and insults toward any group, particularly culturally marginalized groups." Black people find these to be especially prevalent in corporate settings-perhaps due to them being one of the few Black people some of their coworkers ever interact with. This is an especially difficult space for many African Americans. In white corporate spaces Black people are pulled with this dichotomy of remaining who they are at the core, while simultaneously shrinking themselves to fit in- unfortunately making everyone but themselves comfortable. A few examples of some of the microaggressions our white counterparts project, sometimes unknowingly include:

- Hair... hair... The mysteries of Black hair. It's perfectly acceptable to complement or be in awe of Black hair. It is in fact dynamic, and pretty much defies gravity. Regardless, avoid touching it especially without asking, expressing that you prefer another style, asking if our hair 'grew overnight,' because although magical, *that's* simply impossible. Something as plain as not recognizing someone due to a hairstyle change is dismissive, and provides evidence for just how little effort you're putting in. Especially avoid any negative comments or bias toward Black hairstyles. It's a deep-rooted part of our culture, and many of the creative styles are for 'protection' (from breakage etc.) Black hair is complicated, requiring a lot more time and maintenance than you may realize. Lastly, don't use words like 'nappy,'- as any hair may get tangled or matted, only hair from African roots really gets 'nappy.' (and no, that's not a bad thing, just uniquely difficult to manage.) Each of these have been stated to me in various instances- one of the reasons I chose not to settle until I found a corporate space where I was fully accepted. Our hair is still professional even when it's braided, weaved up, or reaching to the sky.

- Skin. Very simply Black skin 'burns' differently- there is a layer of protection due to melanin. (Dark pigmentation protects from DNA damage and absorbs the right amounts of UV radiation needed by the body, as well as protects against folate depletion. Yes, we should still use sunscreen- there's just an inherent difference.) I'm sharing this because in conversations with Black people there is no need to question skin color or voice statements including 'I'm almost 'as dark as you,' with tan. It's usually void of upright intent.

- Implying affirmative action is offensive- we've learned about its origination above. Even if it's meant well, do not express to a Black colleague that they were 'hired due to a quota,' or that 'they'll have an easier time finding a job.' That's simply not true. Ironically, those who've said this to me are white *women-possibly* not realizing they're categorized as a 'diversity hire' as well.

- Raising frivolous questions like 'Are you the intern?' especially after a welcome email has just gone out with details on my position and background. (I may look young, but I'm 30+ :) Instead, just introduce yourself and ask if you're unaware.

- The pay gap for minorities in America is egregious- with Black women making on average 62 cents on the dollar compared to their white male counterparts. Latina and Native women are even less.

- Try to avoid treating Black people as a monolith. We are not all the same. We may not have the 'Black answer.' It's quite a burden to represent every Black person in America. Although we share culture and similarities, We're still very divergent from each one another. Instead, making an attempt to genuinely get to know *that* person will provide a more authentic reflection of Black culture for you to respect and understand.

- Regarding the topic of Black culture, consider the impact it's had on pop culture. Music, fashion, memes, television, dance, comedy, slang, food, sports, general trends. Try to balance consumption with genuine respect and preservation. There's a fine line between this high esteem and appropriation. Take part and appreciate it, but don't center our culture around yourself or use it as a trend, as this essentially erases the people who created it.

- Recognize the magnitude of what we bring to the table. In corporate settings especially, don't speak over us, devalue our ideas, reduce our creativity, or again- just have us around for 'diversity.'

- Pause before you use terms such as: "Cracking the whip." It's offensive and triggering every single time.

- Even small things- that literally associate 'black' with negative, white with positive (white lie, blackballed etc...) stop using them. It has a psychological effect, even unconsciously.

- Outside of a workspace, consider simple things such as travel may bring unnecessarily discomfort for Black people. A vacation requires research to digest the level of racism in other countries; preparing to be stared at, treated as a spectacle, or stumbling into a place where an "anti-black hierarchy of human value is in full effect."

- Shopping. Walking into a retail store, not being greeted- just followed. These things happen regardless of socio-economic status. Oprah was racially profiled in a store in Switzerland, trying to purchase a $38,000 handbag.

- Stores like Anthropologie, here in America actually have a code that's announced each time a Black person enters the store- 'Nick'.

- Lastly, avoid being someone who aggravates, complains, trivially calls the police, and harasses Black and Brown people for simply existing. (Real examples that we've all stumbled upon- having a BBQ at the park, drawing with chalk outside of their own home, living in *their* neighborhood,, etc.. A #Karen) This generation says it best- it's not exhausting being Black, it's actually quite the opposite. It's the world that makes it exhausting.

Public Schooling/Education Inequities:

- This is such a large, expansive, topic- I'd encourage additional research, attention to law, and who we're voting in to make decisions around education.
- Even the manner in which funding is funneled into public schools is discriminatory. The Washington Post reported a $23 Billion funding gap between predominantly white vs. Black schools, often based on the value of local property, tied to the ability of residents to pay higher taxes.
- Children must have their basic needs satisfied before they may even ponder on why they're in school. If they're busy considering where their next meal is coming from, they're likely not concerned with what lovely poetry Shakespeare has written, or how we solve for x.

- For underserved youth- therapy, counseling, alternative ways of learning should be offered. Many of these kids are extraordinarily smart and need to be taught in a manner that best serves them.

- African American Vernacular English must also be recognized as a dual language, as it incorporates its own expressions and rules that are also valid. Educators must remember to celebrate the unique differentiators of Black students rather than exclude or punish them.

- Personally, I've always enjoyed school and reading- but the case could have been much different if I didn't have parents advocating for me. In kindergarten, I was the only Black student in my classroom- my teacher suggested I be held back, not due to my skills or learning ability, but because I was too quiet. Excuses like this are how so many Black students are shuffled into lower level classes, and not given a realistic path to success.

- Examining a similar, yet unconnected occurrence, a close friend's nephew completing kindergarten during a global pandemic has been requested by his teachers to be failed. Not for lack of competence, but simply due to absence of access to materials that would allow him to complete his studies at home. (Often, Black and brown people are hit with classism right along with racism.)

- There are children that don't have access to adequate textbooks or basic learning necessities- let alone a path to college.

- Take for example Kelley Williams-Bolar, a Black mother- sentenced to 3 years & ordered to pay $30k for sending her child to a better school district- one in which she didn't reside.

- Additionally, education reform arrives by reflecting on real, holistic Black African history and its connection to America and the world.

Health Care Inequities:

- A space, especially in America where one should feel secure, and heard- Black people often do not. From the Tuskegee experiment, to Henrietta Lacks. Lead paint experiments, to treating Black patients like guinea pigs.

- Studies have found "African American patients are less likely to receive medical services than White patients with similar complaints and symptoms." This is prevalent especially in America's disparities in childbirth complications.

- The "Father of Gynecology," James Marion Sims notoriously experimented on enslaved Black women without anesthesia.

- Another issue is inadequate bias training among the health care workforce. In their investigation of U.S. maternal mortality, NPR and ProPublica collected more than 200 stories from African American mothers and discovered that "feeling devalued and disrespected by medical providers was a unifying theme. Mothers also frequently reported that medical staff did not take their pain seriously, consistent with earlier studies that found pain is often undertreated in African

American patients." (2-3x more likely to die)

- Consider respected stars like Beyoncé or Serena Williams, still needing to fight

  for their discomfort during childbirth to be recognized.

Pregnancy-related deaths by race in the U.S. in 2018

Number of deaths per 100,000 live births.

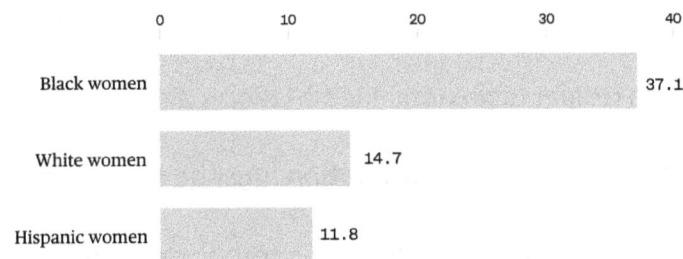

0	10	20	30	40

Black women — 37.1

White women — 14.7

Hispanic women — 11.8

Source: National Center for Health Statistics
Graphic: Jiachuan Wu / NBC News

Environmental Racism

- Black, Native and Latino communities are especially more susceptible to their

  environments being polluted- often by corporate entities.

- The EPA has concluded studies that Black people are more likely to be in areas

  exposed to carcinogenic pollutants. Black people are exposed to 1.5 greater

  anthropogenic particulates than whites, including automobile fumes, smog, soot,

  oil smoke, ash, and construction dust- a contributor to several lung conditions,

  heart attacks, and possible premature deaths. "It seems that almost anywhere

  researchers look, there is more evidence of deep racial disparities in exposure to

  environmental hazards."

- Correlation between locations of heavy industry, oil extraction which leads to higher cancer rates in places like 'Cancer Alley'- along the Mississippi River. Flint water crisis, or Detroit having the most polluted zip code, which happens to be 80% Black.

- Another recent example comes from the small town of Africatown, AL- home to one of the last slave ships to land in America. Their self-sufficiency has been threatened, as residents recently filed a lawsuit against International Paper Company (IPC). They say the corporation must be held accountable for the high levels of dioxins and furans—highly toxic compounds shown to be linked to cancer—into the air, ground, and water in amounts that exceeded EPA limits.

Additional Notes on Equality:

- We also must not forget, even within the Black community that liberation is inclusive of everyone- regardless of sex or identity. Robert Jones Jr. shared it best, "please find a way to heal your trauma and unlearn your indoctrination instead of unleashing it on Black LGBTQIA+ people. Until all Black lives matter, liberation remains out of reach." This community is often left behind in the push for freedoms and reform.

- Let's consider even the minute advantages of being Caucasian. Again, this is no fault of one individual- it's attributed to a system: the benefit of seeing yourself represented everywhere- dolls, movies, commercials, even products like Band-Aids. (Your nude color is not everyone's nude- and not being required to consider this is a privilege in itself, highlighting the simple inequalities Black people and people of color face daily.)

- Recognize exclusion and racism within brands. Imagine you're a Black woman, just for this exercise... In an ad or television commercial, do you see your brown skin? Is it hidden in the back? Cut off by the 30 second commercial limit? Preferred lighter? Is there any Kinky hair? If you are missing; if representation is missing, call them out. Now, as a black woman build up your esteem elsewhere, without the world backing you.

- Don't disregard anyone else's experience, just because it hasn't been your own. Growing up being policed in Black neighborhoods, not adhering to beauty standards of the world and being reminded of it constantly, needing to learn additional rules of survival as a child are often unique to the Black experience.

While attending college in North Carolina, I was driving and realized I was being tailed by an older white man- he was gesturing frantically and wouldn't let up so I pulled over to a gas station to figure out what was going on. He stormed out of the car charged directly at my window, yelling, spewing the N-word, while threatening me with a gun. He threw something at my car and eventually left before I called the police. Turns out he thought I'd been driving too fast in his neighborhood- where my friend and I had just dropped off her younger brother. When the officers did finally respond, they were so nonchalant about the situation because apparently his "license plate was registered in a different county." There was nothing they could do.

I don't consider myself oppressed, but I've experienced oppression. I empathize deeply with the inexorable oppression my people have been wading through. If you've not personally experienced racism, doesn't mean there's not a completely separate world of injustices taking place parallel to your own experience.

PART 5:

AFRICA. PUT SOME RESPECT ON HER NAME

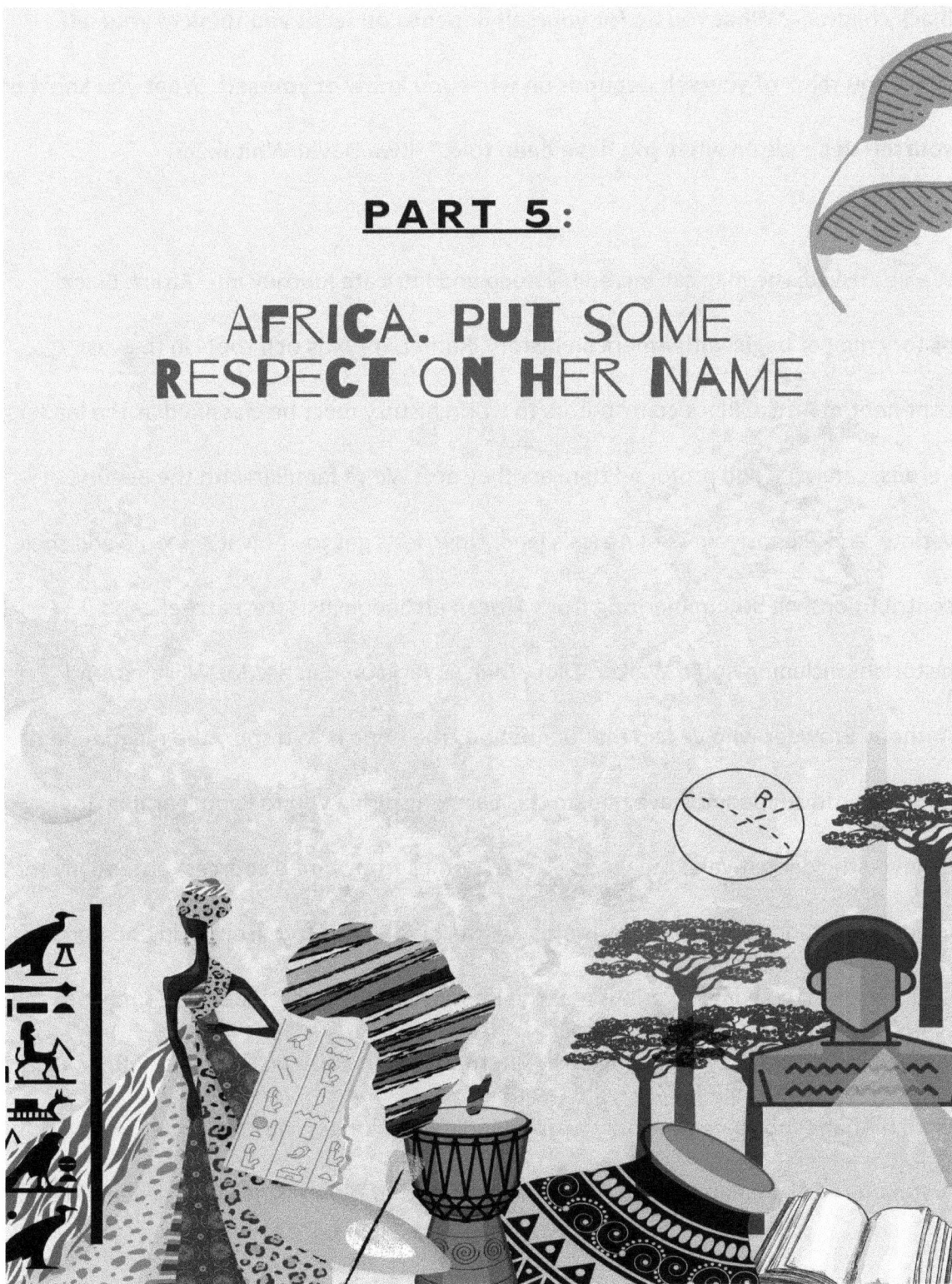

Black children- "What you do for yourself depends on what you think of yourself. What you think of yourself depends on what you know of yourself. What you know of yourself depends on what you have been told." -Kwa David Whitaker

We've arrived; the magical, incredibly deep and intricate journey into Africa. Black history did not begin with American history. Rather, it holds rich roots in the vast continent of Africa. Black contributors to world history must be classified as the leaders, heroes, catalysts, and profound thinkers they are. We're familiar with the beauty, variety, and expansiveness of Africa's land. Now, let's get to know it's people and their contributions. I'll be summarizing from African archaeologists, researchers and historians including Robin Walker, Diop, John G. Jackson, Chancellor Williams, and Anthony Browder who've laid the foundation. The hope is to display the magnitude of influence African people have had on this Earth; inspiring you to keep learning. It's believed the derivative of the word "Africa" comes from varied sources- potentially the Greek word "aphrikē," which translates as "the land that is free from cold and horror." Additionally, it could be a variation of the Roman word "aprica," meaning sunny; or the Phoenician word "afar," meaning dust. Alternatively, in Kemetic History of Afrika, Dr. Cheikh Anah Diop shares the only word of indigenous origin; Africa's ancient name; it's first name of Alkebulan. Alkebu-lan, meaning "mother of mankind" or "garden of Eden."

It was used by the Moors, Carthagenians, Nubians, and Ethiopians; the original people of this continent.

- Kemet and Nubian, are synonymous with the word African. (Same with the word Ethiopian via old text.) The first civilization in Nubia, and in history developed around 3800 BC; the heartland being in the City of Meroe- well known for temples, royal pyramids and an advanced writing system closely resembling hieroglyphics. Ancient Nubia was located in Eastern Africa, right under Egypt. Culturally, Nubia is the "ancestor of Egypt." Just as the people of America today aren't the same as 500 years ago, the original inhabitants of Egypt- were Black. The Nubians were an extremely sophisticated people.

- Egypt, a Nile Valley civilization "was already old before Europe was born." It's important to acknowledge, for the same reason invaders shot off the noses of statues and cultural pieces to disguise Black features, that European historians have deliberately programmed African people out of respectable history. **"History is a compass that people use to find themselves on the map of human geography."** African history is important to know and recognize.

- The oldest monarchy in the world was African, as was the first 12 dynasties in Kemet, also known as ancient Egypt. (3150-1783 BC)

Kemet has had a profound impact on world civilizations:

- **Astronomical knowledge** that came from Kemet included the calendar year, the designation of the second, minute, and hour as measurements of time, plotting movement of the stars, phases of the moon, and identifying planets.

- Various time keeping devices were developed in Kemet to record the passage of time. The word hour is derived from the word Horus (with a meaning representing light, or the rising sun.)

- The Nile Valley people also made significant progress in **aeronautical engineering** (flight), mining, and shipbuilding/travel. A 4,600 year old ship was found near the Great Pyramid of Khufu at Giza. African people have been circumnavigating the globe for centuries.

grandmotherafrica.com

- The Kemet people created and divided the 12 signs of the zodiac- horoscope.

- They first connected these patterns to agriculture, which is critical to acknowledge. Once humans' basic need for food is satisfied, we may focus attention on other supreme philosophical issues including "Who am I, Where did I come from, and what is my reason for being?" Developing agricultural systems based on seasons and the sun's rotation allowed Earth's people to become less

nomadic (transient)- and plant roots to develop civilizations.

Ancient Nubian Pharoah, & Queen Tiye

- Most are aware of Egypt's contributions, at least architecturally. However, history does not always acknowledge their blackness.

- The Kemet/Nubian Black people established and ruled over Egypt for thousands of years providing proud structures including the massive pyramids- defying rules of architecture.

- Nubia was the lifeline of ancient Kemet; the source of its language, philosophy and religion. For over 3,000 years Nubia played a huge role in the development of its daughter nation Kemet. The Kemet people established what we know as Egypt. There were several Nubian Kings and Queens of ancient Nubia

Statutes & inscriptions of Nubian pharaohs & people, found in modern Sudan.

- Queen Tiye, great royal wife of Amenhotep III- one of the greatest Nubian queens to rule over Egypt was excellent at building alliances and known for her diplomacy.

- Archaeological feats accomplished in ancient Egypt amount to no other historical site on earth. According to world renowned Johns Hopkins mathematician Elmer

D. Robinson, "analysis and mathematical modeling of the Great Pyramid indicates that the ancient Egyptians had a knowledge of geometry and mathematics... a level matched only within the last 200 years. Attempts to recreate construction have failed- still raising the question of how the great pyramid was built."

- The Great Sphinx- the largest & oldest monument created out of a single stone- (originally named Her-em-akhet- Heru of the Horizon- positioned where the sun rises.)

- The Tekhenw (or teknen)- the tall pencil-like statue- with modern duplicates found all over the world. (Washington Monument, Rome, Turkey, Germany etc.) Also called Obelisks- they were used to determine the time based on the length of their shadow.

- Pharaohs ruled over ancient Egypt for three millennia- (3150 BC- 31 BC) until Egypt was absorbed by the Roman Empire.

- There were kings, queens, leaders, and teachers called Hersetha who focused on subjects of Heaven/Astronomy. They called themselves Mystery Teachers studying lands (geography), the depths (geology), the secret world (philosophy and theology), even teachers who examined words (law and communication.)

- The center of learning was called Ipet-Isut, intact to help Nile Valley Civilizations understand the relationship between themselves and the universe- the truest sense of the word University.

- One of the most notable teachers, with varied talents was Imhotep- the architect for designing several pyramids. Also brilliant in astronomy, poetry, philosophy, & medicine. He was known as a Super Genius and the world's first Physician- a title later stolen by Greek, Hippocrates (2,200 years later.)

- He wrote one of the oldest medical papers or journals to exist, called the 'Smith Papyrus," which included details such as advanced surgical methods for over 48 different injuries, and details on things like the neurological relationship between the brain/spinal cord/nervous system and the body.

Above: Obelisk in Luxor temple & sculpture of Imhotep
Next Image: The Luxor temple

Connecting History:

- Greece is known as the "birthplace of European civilization," yet credit for the teachings of Plato, Aristotle, Pythagoras etc... is not given to its true source- Egypt. Their learnings absorbed at Egyptian schools (Egyptian Mystery System) were taken in and held as their own ideals.

- The Egyptian Mystery system taught ideals around hymns, hieroglyphics, geography, astronomy, law, medicine, mathematical symbolism, and esoteric philosophy. Some examples that were transferred to Greek Philosophers are: Transmigration (the soul's immortality and salvation), the idea of union of opposites (harmony in the universe,) The Cosmological Doctrine (the entire universe being an arrangement of numbers,) + things like the atom, supreme good, or the Doctrine of Universal flux (constant change within the universe.)

- **Aristotle** for example, was credited with writing over 1,000 books. Aristotle not only took books from the Library of Alexandria (who's source was ancient Egypt), but also received financial aid from Alexander the Great to purchase some. The knowledge he is credited with took Ancient Egypt over 5,000 years to accumulate.

- Connect this even to modern day "borrowed" knowledge, or even culture- like Elvis- literally imitating Black artists, after it was called jungle music- and receiving the fame and credit. Even cornrows, hoop earrings, dances today which are often monetized and credited as a cool part of 'pop' culture once exhibited by someone other than a Black person.

- Ancient Africans experimented with and created chemical, medicinal and surgical sciences, mimicked by the Greeks.

- Greek sources even indicate that "Ethiopians, that is, Black people in general used to inhabit a wide stretch of the ancient world, not just Africa... a considerable tract of Asia was occupied by the Ethiopian race, and the term India was often made to comprise southern Africa.... Ethiopia is frequently made to include southern India. Blacks pioneered civilization by establishing the first trading routes." -Arnold H.L Heeren, German historian

Spirituality:

- There are several spiritual concepts, specifically popular in the Christian faith that have come directly from Ancient Africa, and the 'Book of the Coming Forth by Day:' everlasting life, God molding man from clay and breathing breath into him, the concept of good and evil, a soul going to heaven, the holy trinity, immaculate conception and resurrection. There were 42 laws- several strikingly similar to the 10 commandments. Interestingly enough it's said that Moses, of Africa received theological studies from Akhenaton- the Pharaoh married to

Queen Nefertiti, brother of King Tutankhamen. (Who also helped bring the idea of a singular personification of 'God.')

- Let's take one simple concept from ancient Nubia: **Amon,** a Necher (not a god, just an integral part of that which is God)- they believed to be omnipresent, the 'hidden one,' to have neither beginning or end. It's morphed into the word we still say to conclude prayers- Amen.

- The Ankh (pronounced 'Unk') - symbolizes life or breath of life and is formed to symbolize female fertility. Also symbolizing immortality and the universe.

- Spirituality in Africa has also been the basis of some in the Caribbean, and South America- notably **Yoruba-** a blend of powerful ancestral connection, indigenous beliefs, proverbs, and spiritual concepts.

- Ashe is the energy found in all natural things. A powerful life force possessed by humans and divine beings alike.

- Oshun is the goddess of love, beauty, fertility.

- Yemaya- a goddess representative of nature's elements- an original 'mother earth'- nourishing, gentle energy, especially strong near water.

Photo: Ankh, Yemeya

Semi-Modern African Empires and Expansion:

- Even down to the discovery of the Americas- there is strikingly obvious evidence

  of black civilizations- even down to the Seventeen Olmec heads in Mexico.

  African words in the native American languages, negro faces on vases and bowls,

  African foods like peanuts or yams, as well as totemism similar to those practiced

  in Africa. Africans began appearing in the Americas between 1160-580 BCE.

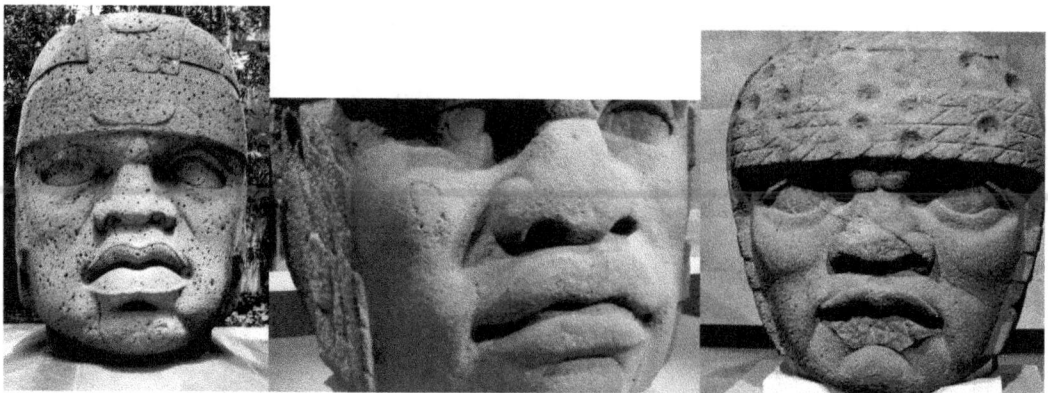

- African history proceeded without interruption up until about the sixth century, Nubia remained a sole source of culture and civilization.

- Even Arabic script used in many of the civilizations of west Africa and central Sahara was in fact of African origin- invented by Abul Aswan. There were European translation centers of Moorish and Arabic texts, established in the 10th centuries which by the 12th and 13th centuries contributed to a rise of major European Universities.

- Throughout history, thriving civilizations all over Africa that many are not familiar with: Carthage, northern Africa (modern day Tunisia)- known for robust exploration, maintaining that they crossed to America. Very rich and opulent. There were miles of towering walls, public restaurants, libraries, baths, garbage collectors, lavish homes.

- Hannibal- possibly Carthage's best-known figure- one of the greatest military commanders in world history

- Other notable civilizations include Aksumite Empire (4th c. BCE - 1st c. BCE) and later the Ethiopian Empire (1270-1974) ruled by a series of monarchs. Haile

Selassie, the last Emperor of Ethiopia, was deposed in a coup d'état. The Yoruba in Nigeria- admired by scholars as a beautiful walled and paved city rich in metals, bronze, gold, and pottery art. (some have linked Yoruba culture with ancient America.)

- Kumasi was the capital of the Asante Kingdom, 10th century-20th century. "Promenades and public squares, cosmopolitan lives, exquisite architecture and everywhere spotless and ordered, a wealth of architecture, history, prosperity and extremely modern living" – PD Lawton

- Two story homes were timber-framed with walls of lath and plaster construction, and indoor, even upstairs toilets. A 'tree of life' always stood in the courtyard which was the central point of a family compound.

- European travelers described the people of **Kongo** as "dressed in silk, civilized to the marrow of their bones."

- Benin also flourished in art and was known for strong leadership and military power. The Wall, or vast system of defensive walling was over 10,000 miles, actually gaining an entry into the modern Guinness book of Records. Travelers have said "these people are in no way inferior to the Dutch as regards cleanliness; they wash and scrub their houses so well that they are polished and shining like a looking-glass."

- **Gao-** a Songhai city became very powerful, known for trading- attracting merchants from Morocco, Tunis, and Egypt. It was colorful and vibrant until it was looted for its treasures- artillery and guns supplied by Queen Elizabeth of England.

- The **Songhai** people were known for being highly intelligent, industrious, and great traders and warriors.

Artwork by Leo and Diane Dillo

- The Swahili States- including Kenya, Somalia, Tanzania, Zanzibar and Mozambique flourished from aprox. 700-1505 AD. Extraordinarily skilled workers in metal and distinguished as traders- it was documented in the 12th century by Al Idrissi that East Africans had been making steel for more than 1,500 years. Also known for opulence, they were known to be finely clad in rich garments of silk and cotton.

- Zimbabwe, in southern Africa was a center of crafts as well as industry where gold, copper and iron were minded and worked. Builders were said to have highly sophisticated mathematical & astronomical knowledge as well as engineering skills. The Mutapa (king) had a standing army of 100,000 men, with 300,000 to be mobilized if needed. This, along with 6,000 Amazons- or female soldiers. They'd also had sophisticated systems of money and resources set aside for the disadvantaged, including land and food designated to them at public cost.

A Golden Age:
- There were **modern empires in Ghana**- known as the "Land of Gold," These West African empires included Mali and Songhai, which was the size of the entire continent of Europe.

- **Mali's** most famous leader was Mansa Musa (coming to power in 1312) building one of the greatest empires of the time- still known as the richest man to ever live, amassing an estimated worth of $400 Billion- acquiring his wealth from the production and trade of salt and gold; more than half of the world's supply at the time.

- Musa fulfilled a lengthy pilgrimage to Mecca in 1324 with a caravan of 60,000 people, carrying so much gold and spending so lavishly that the price of gold fell in those lands for ten years following.

- Mali was also home to Timbuktu- the richest city of it's time, often called the "Paris of Medieval Times." Timbuktu was an important stop in the trans-Saharan trade route, becoming a major center in gold, salt, and ivory, in the 14th century. Also housing one of the oldest universities (that still stands); it was known to be a golden source of learning, providing scholarships to over tens of thousands of students who traveled from various places around the world. Factories flourished, and there were a great number of judges, doctors, clerics within the city.

- Witnesses came from several parts of the world and documented. One account from Italian art and architecture scholar, Sergio Domian stated the following regarding his visit: "Thus was laid the foundation of an urban civilization. At the height of its power, Mali had at least 400 cities, and the interior of the Niger Delta was very densely populated." Timbuktu alone had a 14th century population of 115,000 - five times larger than medieval London.

- Many old West African families have private library collections that go back hundreds of years. Following are pages from Timbuktu manuscripts outlining mathematics and astronomy:

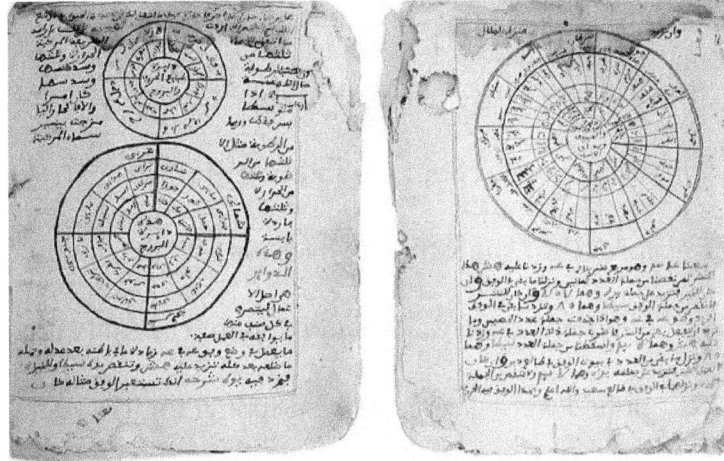

- There are over 700,000 surviving books, written in Mande, Suqi, Fulani, Timbuktu, and Sudani. The manuscripts include readings on math, medicine, poetry, law and astronomy- used as the first encyclopedias, in the 14th century before the Europeans got the idea later in the 18th century.

- A current examination of these manuscripts by Michael Palin, in his TV series 'Sahara,' concludes Timbuktu, Mali has produced "a collection of scientific texts that clearly show the planets circling the sun. They date back hundreds of years.

This convincing evidence shows that the scholars of Timbuktu knew a lot more than their counterparts in Europe. In the fifteenth century in Timbuktu, the mathematicians knew about the rotation of the planets, knew about the details of the eclipse. They knew things which we had to wait for 150 almost 200 years to know in Europe when Galileo and Copernicus came up with these same calculations and were given a very hard time for it."

- Mali's founder as well as most influential leader, Sundiata Keita laid the foundation for a powerful and wealthy African empire and created one of the first charters of human rights, the **Manden Charter.** Also known as the Kouroukan Fouga, it speaks on peace within a diverse nation, free slavery, while full of education, and food security among other things.

- Elam was a mighty negro civilization of Persia- flourishing around 2900 BC

- Sumer was the first civilization to appear in Asia (also named Chaldaea and Mesopotamia by the Greeks.) The term 'Afro-Asian' still exists today, in Asia. There are stark features that exist in modern African tribes of certain areas, and original people from small islands, to countries like Australia.

San grandmother and her granddaughter. San people of the Kalahari desert and Southern Africa.

Other **Ancient African Women to admire**: Queen Amina with her walls of protection, Empress Makeda or Queen of Sheba- mentioned in the Bible and Quran, she was one of the most powerful women of her time, controlling the Red Sea, an enormous trade route. Queen Neith-Hotep- began Egypt's first golden age. Nefertiti- enigmatic, known for her beauty. Tawosret- another female pharaoh. Amanirenas- a kushite one-eyed warrior queen, who fought off Roman invasion in the first century AD. + let this inspire you to dig into Black women of America that we may have skipped over in history class as well.

Middle Image: Painting of Queen of Sheba, & last image- sculpture of Queen Amina

- It should be noted that **Women** have always been revered with positions of power in several parts of Africa. The fields are cultivated by women, the female menstrual cycle was the first timekeeper in history- linking it to the lunar month. Women are seen as the Primal mother... giver of life...symbol of purity, yet a destroyer... blessed rainmaker, herbalist, healer, warrior of Amazonic fierceness... protector of man... huntress and dancer..."

"For far too long, a majority of Africans have been indifferent to misrepresentations about who they are." — Childo Nwangwu

The African Diaspora is usually referred to when referencing geographic areas Black people were taken during the slave trade. However, there's a diaspora that exists from the thousands of years of African migration around the globe- Asia, India, South America, Australia, small islands etc... Here are a few photos dedicated to their resilience, diversity and beauty:

© Photo Maurice ASCANI

Tuareg people of the Sahel & Sahara, Lagos man, Ethiopian man, Fulani woman, Dravidian people

African Models @Lagosfashionweek

PART 6:

'MODERN' EUROPEAN COLONIZATION

AFRICA'S RESISTANCE & THE IMPACT

Modern' European Colonization, Africa's Resistance and the

Impact:

- Looking into areas of history that are heavily studied, such as the European dark ages, there are omissions of African influence. After being denied learning, reading, and education, knowledge was escorted back to parts of Europe by Black 'Moorish' conquests. Moors were Black Africans, often Muslim also; called Blackamoors, or Berbers. An Arab chronicler also described Moorish Emperor Yusuf ben-Tachfin as "a brown man with wooly hair."

- In a time where Christian Europe was 99% illiterate, with classical manuscripts and documents disappearing, several were preserved and copied by the Moors. The only two libraries that were allowed in the world at the time were in Africa.

- **Tarik Ibn Zayid** (above left) led a Moorish army of 300 Arabs and 6700 Africans in a battle conquering Spain around 700 A.D- erecting architecture that still stands today, the introducing paper, new clothing styles, foods, hygiene products, irrigation systems, and attention to mathematics, medicine, and the physical sciences.

- The most significant Moorish musician was known as **Ziryab**, aka the Blackbird who arrived in Spain in 822. His musical contributions are staggering, laying the early groundwork for classical Spanish music.

- He was also known as a polymath with knowledge in astronomy, geography, meteorology, botanica, cosmetics, culinary art and fashion. Ziryab revolutionized the court at Córdoba and made it the stylistic capital of its time.

- The Moors introduced many new crops including the orange, lemon, peach, apricot, fig, sugar cane, dates, ginger and pomegranate as well as saffron, sugar cane, cotton, silk and rice which remain some of Spain's main products today.

- It was through Africa that the new knowledge of China, India, and Arabia reached Europe.

- They ruled, even as royalty in parts of Europe- primarily Spain and Portugal. With universal education, public libraries, lined streets, again, they helped usher the continent of Europe out of nearly 1,000 years of intellectual and technological disarray.

A Moorish structure in Spain, still erect today.

- Even the visual size of Africa is distorted. It's much larger in reality than they appear on the traditional maps. To the right, there's an outline of just how many large countries can comfortably fit into this continent:

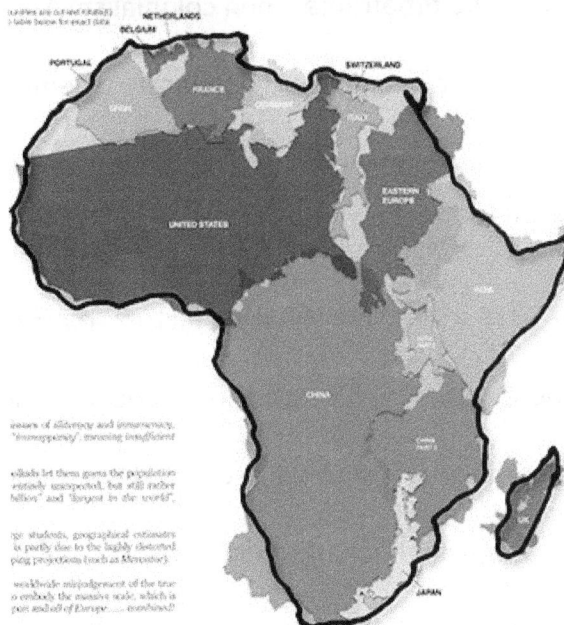

- Areas further North and South of the equator get stretched out: while the ones in the middle get compressed. It may be no accident that the general acceptance of the Mercator projection map corresponds to the inflation it provides to the world's more prosperous nations.

- When piecing these things together, it's important to remember that racist ideologies played a big role in distorting perceptions. Museums were financed and controlled by those who believed the white man's superiority was essentially a religion. Examining ideologies today; paired with ignorance, the media places a heaviness on Black crime, Black victims, Black criminals, Black suspects, Black negative stereotypes; showcasing images of Black death for your consumption.

- Shifting back into the timeframe when colonialism and enslavement began to sweep over Africa, the people were deliberately hemmed in from various directions. Many were survivors- finding solace in places of extreme isolation; often losing their civilization while choosing freedom.

- Noting, there were several contributing factors to African nations being overtaken. There was a "highly humane" aspect of African warfare- where rather than terminate, the goal was to scare off or show dominance. Additionally, there was a belief that the land belongs to no one- it's God's gift to mankind. For those that argue Africans exchanged their own people as slaves, this was only partially correct. The leaders who have agreed were under the assumption that this was servitude, not generation-long, traumatic chattel-slavery.

- The European invaders- who often took over a country based on their own fabricated guise of bringing Christianity to the people, were supported by almost limitless wealth amassed from these exploited people.

- Controlling world education, science, blotting out Black influence, and topping it off with a swift dominance of laws and media- there becomes a very methodical system centered on white supremacy.

- You've learned about some of its origins, like "Social Darwinism" in school. False narratives that perpetuate the myth of Europeans being superior. Again, this provided an automated scapegoat for enslavement, dismantling of culture, ruin and genocide.

- There were other European influences that perpetuated racist stereotypes. David Hume, early 1700s stated: "I am apt to suspect the Negroes, and in general all other species of men to be naturally inferior to the whites. There never was a civilized nation of any other complexion than white." He was ignorant of any of the ancient Black civilizations and contributions ranging from the alphabet, to mining, to the mathematical formulas that laid the foundation for inventions including rocketry and computer science. This ignorance was detrimental.

- Some pieces also simply just do not connect- In 1630, Archbishop James Ussher announced the world- the entire world, was created by God in 4004 BC- this estimate was widely accepted for a couple hundred years. However, the people of Africa were thriving in a highly developed civilization long before then.

- A great majority of the world's people are Black or brown. Ensuring we're not mistaken- just because they have been treated like *'savages'* does not mean in any way that they were.

(Aboriginal Australians being treated extraordinarily inhumanely by European colonizers)

Readers who identify as white, let's check in. Have you been examining yourself- your preconceived notions? Realizing that just as a baby cannot tell an elder about their life, neither should you to your Black peers. Turn your 'we don't see sentiments into 'I see you as a Black person, I understand your Black experience is varied, and different than my own, and your Black life matters.' OluTimehin Adegbeye of modern Nigeria, shares analysis based on her worldly travels that racism is often "people acting normally in a system that promotes and protects Eurocentric power by denying, and at best bracketing the humanity of Africans and Afro-descendant people… In this world, you don't have to be a racist to be racist; it's racist to just passively allow racism to continue." I'd like to share an additional clip from her write up, titled "What is Racism-" giving her the space to fully identify, and provide a path towards living as an Anti-Racist:

- "Anti-blackness is the pivot on which racism turns…. As people – as human beings – we should be able to move through the world, enjoying the same socio-economic resources and freedoms that all human beings deserve."

- "It is not enough to like, befriend, marry, or otherwise interact nicely with Black people… To be anti-racist is actively to promote Black safety, Black prosperity, Black health, Black innocence, Black freedom, Black wellbeing and Black life."

It's imperative to recognize how this attitude has permitted the idea of white supremacy to run rampant. While attempting to conquer various indigenous people, European invaders have traditionally arrived with a superior attitude. Rather than recognize the "rightful owners of the land," they've followed a so called "Caucasian Creed," which became an excuse for destruction and unwarranted slaughter. It essentially stated that the lowest social and economic class of Europeans were superior to the greatest Black King. Other terms that justified the numerous genocides against non-European people was the myth of "manifest destiny," and "divine white right." When indeed these African people were already enlightened, civilized and worshipping one almighty God. They used Christianity as a primary reason to take control of most of the continent of Africa, India, the Caribbean Islands, and both South and North America.

- The Catholic Church greenlit modern slavery. Sir John Hawkins, the first slave-ship captain to bring African slaves to the Americas, was a religious man who encouraged his crew to "serve God daily" and "love one another." This ship was called "The Good Ship Jesus." (One must decipher and know God for themselves; as man may twist a religion to his liking.)

- We must remember that before this shift and transition in religious attitude, many throughout the world worshiped a Black Madonna and child, aka Virgin

Mary. Parts of the world received much of their original spiritual connection from Africa, only to try to cheaply sell it back to them.

- For every two million Black humans enslaved, over a million died.

- The modern slave system was handled like a brokerage system. If someone bought twenty slaves at the beginning of the week, and found themselves short, they'd auction them off, completely dismantling families.

- An account written by a capturer describes the slave trails in Africa as riddled with skeletons and bodies as people stumbled and ran in fear, often succumbing to death by suicide, babies deliberately smothered to avoid a life of captivity.

- There was also a huge fight put up by many- notably **Queen Nzinga**- the most powerful leader against the Portuguese armies, who she fought for forty years. Located in Ndongo- current Angola, she vehemently denied their deceitful tricks, as well as gracefully reacted to their 'Caucasian arrogance.' She used groups of her own soldiers to infiltrate the Portuguese 'Black armies' they'd develop to easily accomplish take over. By doing so it made their usual strategy of internal subversion nearly impossible due to the soldier's loyalty to the queen. The solidarity of the Black people remained unbroken. They created coded drum messages that spread throughout the land, decoded only by those who could understand them as news that guerrilla attacks were being directed by Queen Nzinga. She was raising an army of liberation.

- When Christopher Columbus came to America he didn't actually discover a thing. In total, it's estimated that there were over 56 Million native people eradicated by violence, or as a result of foreign disease.

- Columbus' voyage was considered dangerous, as Europeans still considered the world to be flat. There were explorers of African descent who'd made this voyage time and time again. He was accompanied on this trip by **Pedro Nino**, an African of the Moorish empire which was coming to an end in Spain. Also known as "El Negro." Pedro Nino was the pilot of Columbus' ship the "Santa Maria."

- Slavery was exacerbated by the discovery of the new world and desire to build it up. It became the first major international, multi-country major investment in capital. Scores of Europeans invested in ships, as well as goods and services taken from African countries," making them independently wealthy while destroying and ravaging the largest continent on Earth.

- Not every white person in America is directly related to a slave owner, and certainly not responsible. However, descendant or not, each does still benefit from the systems set in motion. Consider every Black American is affected as well, at some level. The vast majority of Black people you see here in the U.S. are descendants of slaves.

- Although a breathtakingly large number of Africans came here, North America encompassed only about 3%-5% of the total number of slaves transferred throughout the middle passage.

- Other areas that Africans were taken to are called the African Diaspora.

- Countries in the Trans-Atlantic African Diaspora include Brazil, Haiti, Columbia, Dominican Republic, France, Venezuela, Jamaica, Mexico etc...

- Take El Salvador for instance. Through colonization by Europe, cacao, sugar indigo plantations, and mining operations created a strong demand for imported slave labor. The declining native American population had an influence on the Royal Ordinance issued in 1541 which provided Spanish landowners and miners permission to import African slaves into El Salvador. Over the next seventy-five years upwards of 10,000 Africans were brought to work on the haciendas and the mines of El Salvador. Many died without leaving descendants; others however they did leave their ethnic and cultural imprint upon the mixed population.

im·pe·ri·al·ism

/imˈpirēəˌlizəm/

Noun

a policy of extending a country's power and influence through diplomacy or military force

- The thriving ancient cities mentioned above are just a few of the at least 100 African cities destroyed by Europeans.

- No nation ever has actually invaded another society other than to exploit that nation for its own resources.

- There was a literal scramble for Africa.

a. First, Europeans were searching for easily accessible **natural resources**.

Most of the easily accessible resources in Europe had been used up in the initial Industrial Revolution. In order to keep progress moving, Europeans needed new deposits. In Africa, Europeans found vast quantities of coal, iron ore, copper, gold, silver, and most important to the second half of the Industrial Revolution, **rubber**. Some of the largest deposits of rubber were found in the Congo region of central Africa. This became a huge catalyst for conflict in Africa for the last 100 plus years.

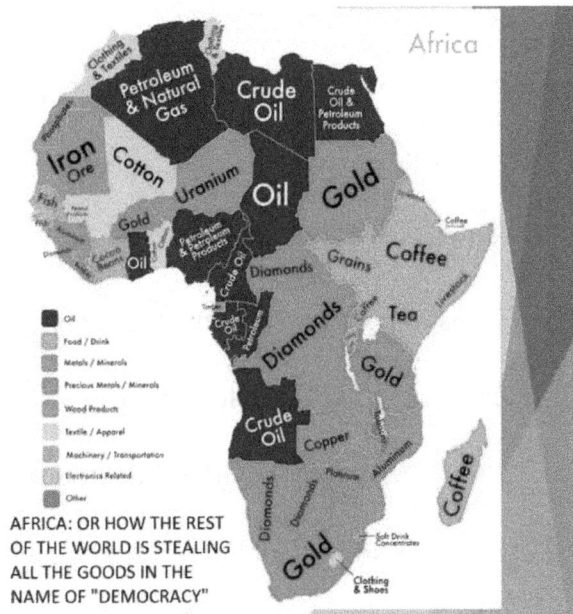

AFRICA: OR HOW THE REST OF THE WORLD IS STEALING ALL THE GOODS IN THE NAME OF "DEMOCRACY"

- Colonization has developed into a sustainable flood of resources into 'Western,' & European countries.

- Looting has always occurred in Africa, upon discovery by outside forces; whether for the people, or the resources. Gold and treasure, then slaves, and finally the plundering for additional resources.

- As the Industrial Revolution was booming, Europe required more materials- so they went to Africa.

- Rubber, used in everything from paints and adhesives, to electrical cables and artificial hearts, is the source of an enormous amount of discord and conflict in places like the Congo.

- The Berlin Conference of 1884 essentially allowed European leaders to sit down and plan out how they would carve out Africa how they saw fit.

- As mentioned, nearly every major, thriving city in Africa was destroyed- whether gradually or swift. This was accompanied by an unrelenting genocide of its people, who were seen as disposable.

- An estimated 5.4 million people were killed in the Congo genocide, led by Belgium's King Leopold. If they weren't killed, he was notorious for chopping off limbs if they didn't work hard enough.

- The beautiful city of Kumasi was blown up, destroyed by fire, and looted by the British at the end of the 19th century.

- In 1897, Benin City was destroyed by British forces, under Admiral Harry Rawson. The city was looted, blown up and burnt to the ground.

- The Germans massacred the Mahi-Mahi people in East Africa.

- The Anglo-Zulu war is another example. In 1879, England found the largest diamond deposit in the world, and waged war eventually taking over and imposing their will over the people of the Zulu area, or South Africa.

- There was much pushback- whether attempting to shut down trade, or block missionaries; some also choose a military option. It was clear most African leaders did not want to surrender their nations to Europe. In 1895, the King of Mossi (modern day Burkina Faso) told the French colonial officer: "I know the whites wish to kill me in order to take my country, and yet you claim that they will help me to organize my country. But I find my country good just as it is. I have no need of them. I know what is necessary for me and what I want: I have my own merchants: also, consider yourself fortunate that I do not order your head to be cut off. Go away now, and above all, never come back."

- The "Mossi States," separate but adjacent to the Mali and Songhai empires, were one of the final to withstand outside rule. They were industrious, dominant powers who resisted conquest for 500 or so years, until being overwhelmed by France in the 20th Century.

- Gold. Oil. Cotton. Iron. Coffee. Petroleum. Diamonds. Tea. Livestock. Textiles. Colton- the mineral that's mined to power your iPhone. These are all found in Africa. When refined, coltan becomes metallic tantalum, a heat-resistant powder that can hold a high electrical charge - crucial for the miniature circuit boards that power our smartphones, laptop computers, pagers and many other high-tech devices. The men who mine this material are underpaid, overworked, and often subject to dangerous- even war-torn working conditions.

- There was one country that was able to completely resist European Imperialism; Ethiopia. King Menelik II ruled the Shoa region in central Ethiopia. During Menelik's rise to power, the Italians allied with him and began supplying Ethiopia with weapons in hopes that Menelik would eventually surrender his power to them. Menelik built an army of 100,000 and pushed back against the Italians after they declared Ethiopia was under their control. On March 1, 1896, the Italians invaded Ethiopia from their neighboring colony of Eritrea. Led by King Menelik, his army offered a conclusive defeat against the Italians at the Battle of Adwa. It was the first time in history that an African army had defeated a European army. Ethiopia has continued to maintain its sovereignty.

Separate photos of Menelik II, born 1844. Ruled Ethiopia from 1889 to his death in 1913

It's quite obvious once you learn the truth of Africa and its greatness, that there has been a massive, co-conspiratorial effort by the "conquerors" to hide, dismantle, and undermine the status of this continent and its people. A Eurocentric view of history teaches us that Europe offered civilization to Africa; or worse- completely omits Africa from the conversation. We know this to be "a complete inversion of the truth," and actually quite laughable when you realize our entire modern society has been built off of colonization and imperialism, justified by racism. The invention and pervasive nature of racism has upheld these ideals for centuries- intertwining itself so deeply into society and the human psyche that it's become almost inescapable. This is what's meant, in a nutshell when it's expressed that "racism is systemic."

Introduction to the Writer:

Adrienne aka Adrie, a proud Alum of North Carolina A&T State University; grew up in a military family in the Baltimore, MD area. Other than writing and highlighting greatness, I'm into fashion, basketball, art, traveling and most importantly being an Aunt to my favorite kids back in North Carolina.

Residing in Los Angeles with my fiancé, who's been an incredible source of love and support for me, I also work full-time as a Director of Partnerships in the Media Industry. Part-time, I'm constantly writing, creating, researching, reading, shopping or finding a new LA nook to explore. I'm working on my second book centered on career, self-love and manifestation. I hope to make an impact and help guide someone into becoming the best version of themselves. Feel free to contact me on how we may connect.

adrie@bronzedmoon.com

@adrie_d

Writer's Note:

The goal I had in mind in crafting this book is to leave the reader wanting more; in awe of Black resilience and contributions, with a gnawing desire to spread the word. The ultimate objective would be to further integrate Afro-centric teachings into the American school system so that it becomes more balanced. It should become apparent that Africans- ancestors of Black Americans have a much deeper history; more than how we were treated here in America. Our history impacts the entire world. It's important to insert this into education, as we're working to dismantle this idea of white supremacy. Thus, ensuring that especially Black children see themselves in history; knowing that they are equally impactful. Amplify Black voices, take action to bring down these systems upholding a false standard of white supremacy; listen, and make space for Black people. Educate yourself, so we may give our children better sources for them to uncover truths.

For myself, the need to enlighten was already brewing; but as with several issues, the Black Lives Matter uprisings have amplified the desire for immediate exposure and empathy. This moment is allowing people to awaken and ascend- with knowledge, clarity, understanding, and a realization of their own power. We have a collective ability to make a real difference, each of us has an important role to play. My hope is that the reader feels armed with a piece of information you may have been unaware of; something you may share; a foundation to hold you up, remind you of how far you've come, and why we must keep fighting. Knowing your worth is the greatest tool to begin advancing and defeating your enemy. Knowledge is a tool that rips down walls, obscurities, and inequities. When we're unified; and activated at a level of collective consciousness, we'll inevitably advance.

"Man has two educations- that which he is given, and the other which he gives himself." -Carter G. Woodson (The Miseducation of the Negro)

My writing 'soundtrack': 🎶 🎵 A "Music for the Movement" Playlist I made- some of my

favorite Black American resistance/inspirational songs for pushing change & fueling the

resistance. (*One of my favorites is Beyoncé's Black Parade")

Please go, in the spirit of 'Sankofa'- move forward while looking back. Turn around and pull someone up. Share knowledge so that you each may find a more clear reflection of yourselves.

Articles and Resources:

Full active links included in Digital copy

Resources to take action from:

1. Check out this List of "86 Angelic Troublemakers to Reset America" Get to know them

2. Learn your Roots, identified down to the tribe with AfricanAncestry.com

3. Shop Black. Lists from Etsy Black, Beyonce's List, Black Owned Everything, Official Black Wall Street, We Buy Black, The Nile, Buy it Black, Shoppe Black, Black Owned Brooklyn, Travel Black w/ TravelNoire.com curated African Travel experiences. Black Owned Restaurant Finder App

4. Educate your Kids with resources like a Book Subscription Box centered on Black kids stories, or Store.urbanintellectuals.com -adult & kid friendly Black history flashcards

5. Read through additional sources below, & share. Find new spaces for Black stories like Journal.Singlestory.org Short Stories & Poetry from people in the African Diaspora. (& book recco's below)

6. Bank Black & Learn about building equity, & wealth to pass along (Finance bloggers here & here- my favorite: TheBudgetnista

Sources:

Archives.gov

Project here (2014 publishing- stats are reflective of this date)

"But Slavery Was so long ago" zerflin

Adinkrabrand

Legacy of Trauma: Context of the African American Existence

Pitchfork.com (Andre 3000 photo)

"Liberty & Slavery- the Paradox of America's Founding Fathers" movie

Elaine Massacre NYT The Forgotten History of America's Worst Racial Massacre Nan Elizabeth Woodruff

Independent.co.uk Details of transatlantic slave voyages The Forgotten History of America's Worst Racial Massacre

Blackwestchester.com Arkansas massacre

LynchinginAmerica.eji.com- (Large, comprehensive report on Lynching in America)

Eji.org Incarceration costs

Black Lives Matter Movement Recap Video @jazminseyes

Nytimes.com here on massacre

Face2faceafrica.com here

Brookings.edu here

NCpedia.com here

Mydailynews.com civil rights pic

Smithsonianmag.com civil rights pic

TheCorrespondent.com What Racism Really Is

Artmuseum.mtholyoke.edu Mlk pic

withoutbullshit.com (systemic & systematic racism)

Nationalpartnership.org (pay gap)

Theatlantic.com (Affirmative action & the myth of Reverse Racism)

Britannica.com

Theundefeated.com Malcolm X

Wubr.org here on redlining

Forbes.com "Bob Johnson's 2% Solution)

Thehill.com here on breonna taylor

Rollingstone.com here on killed BLM leaders

African-americaninventors.org

History.com (Sims, father of Gynecology experiment on Black Women)

Invent.org

Opseu.gov (Social Justice ally)

cnn.com

Overt/Covert White supremacy chart @theconciouskid Safehouse Progressive Alliance for Nonviolence (2005). Adapted: Ellen Tuzzolo (2016)

Biography.com here

Lawenforcementmuseum.org Police originated as Slave Patrols

mirror.co/uk Britain paying slave owners

Prisonpolicy.org

Vera.com price of prisoners

Sentencingproject.org here

Schoolhistory.co.uk Slave whippings

Vox.com How Slavery Became America's First Big Business

BusinessInsider.com Monuments Built by Slaves

Psmag.com America, The House that Slavery Built

Institute for policy studies (cia, drugs Black neighborhoods)

Ranker.com companies using prison labor

Youth Transferred to the Adult Criminal Justice System

Bustle.com (Prison Industrial Complex)

Wbur.org Prison labor- California fires

Vox.com here cost of incarceration

Goodmenproject.com (cost prison vs. education)

Wikipedia.com (microaggressions definition)

Nytimes.com "Yes We mean literally abolish the police"

Statistica.com here

SmithsonianMag.org History of Police in America

Mappingpoliceviolence.org Tracked Police Killings & violence

Npr.org oprah racial profiling

Marketplace.org Militarizing Police

Vice.com Baltimore Police Planting Fake Guns on Shooting Victims

Aclu.org Marijuana arrests

Theguardian.com

Therealnews.com here -johns hopkins health experiments

Nih.gov here

Americanprogress.org AA Women maternal disparities

Nbcnews.com Black women birth healthcare

Time.com here

Mappingpoliceviolence.org

theOutline.com - guilty plea's here

The Case for Reparations - Ta Nehisi Coates

What is Owed - Nikole Hannah Jones

Prisonpolicy.org

newsone.com

Quora.com

Thecut.com Anthropologie, retail racism

Forbes.com 2% solution by Billionaire Robert Smith

Nytimes.com You want a Confederate Monument? My Body is a Confederate Monument

Memphistours.co/uk Luxor temple

Thefunambulist.net -Slave Ship

Legaciesunfolding.blogspot.com African Explorers and Settlers of the New World

WashingtonPost.com (Inequity- funding public schools)

Nytimes.com Netflix Moves 100 Million in Deposits to Bloster Black Banks

TheHill.com (mother jailed due to child's school district)

@futureearth environmental racism

TheAtlantic.com environmental racism

Quartz.com environmental racism

https://www.brainyquote.com/topics/society-quotes

Blackhistory.neocities.org African contributions to society & noses broken off monuments

Guardian.ng Africa's Original Name

Corespirit.com African Cities that were Completely Destroyed by Europeans

Face2faceafrica.com (Timbuktu)

Ancient.eu Timbuktu

Atlasobscura.com (Timbuktu Manuscripts)

Smithsonianmag.com Mansa Musa

Nobility-association.com African Monarchy's

Ancient Nubia

Ancient-origins.net

Finance-monthly.com mansa musa worth

Hubpages.com Black Moors in Europe

realhistoryww.com 'Ancient man & his first Civilizations' (Historians changing Egyptian statues)

More on Ancient Egypt

Africans in Asia

Alaraapothocary.com (Benin)

Sudanforam.net (modern African woman/child pic)

African photos

Kiafriqa.com Moors in Europe- contributions

Blackhistory.com Moors

Atlantablackstar.com Moors

A-Z list of even more African Legends

Rarehistoricalphotos.com (Aboriginal Australians)

Theperspective.org Olmec heads

Aljazeera.com (Conference of Berlin)

https://slavevoyages.org/

Dailymail.co.uk (colton mining)

Blackfacts.com

Orderwhitemoon.com Yemeya

Explainthisstuff.com (rubber use)

Worldatlas.com

Amandala.com (El Salvador Black exclusion)

Theguardian.com (Genocide in Congo)

Congoresources.com

Singlestory.org African Empires

Nationalgeographic.com Sundiata

Visibilityofcolor.tumblr.com Queen Amina

Allthatsinteresting.com Queen Nzinga

webs.bcp.org (Africa's response to Imperialism)

Nbcelarn.com (Emperor Menalik of Ethiopia)

Wikipedia.com (Emperor Menalik of Ethiopia)

Learnreligions.com Yoruba

360here.com Africa on the map

Vice.com Yoruba/Oshun

Theculturetrip.com Seychelles pics

Alientlaw.com Nigerian city pics

Ancient.eu Ankh

@lagosfashionweek

Ethiopian model @iam_queenroe

Kamdora.com street style

Canva.com

Blanckdigital.com Lagos street style

Cnn.com African movie

Essence.com Kenyan wedding

Ozy.com Modern news resource
Timbuktutravel.com Top African Fashion Designers
Pbs.org The Meaning of Fourth of July for the Negro
Nytimes.com The Case for Black with a Capital B

"Nile Valley Contributions to Civilization Vol 1"- Anthony Browder
"Ethiopia and the Origin of Civilization" -John G. Jackson
"Introduction to African Civilization" -John G. Jackson
"Ancient Egypt. The Light of the World. Vol II" -Gerald Massey
"Civilization or Barbarism- An Authentic Anthropology"- Cheikh Anta Diop
"How White Folks Got So Rich. The Untold Story of American White Supremacy" -
Reclamation Project
"Stolen Legacy- Greek Philosophy is Stolen Egyptian Philosophy" - George G.M. James
"The Destruction of Black Civilization"- Chancellor Williams
"When We Ruled" -Robin Walker
"They Came Before Columbus"- Ivan Van Sertima

Additional Books & Resources:
1619 Podcast on American Slavery by NYT
Anti Racist Classroom
"How to be an Anti-Racist" Ibram x Kendija
"The New Jim Crow" Michelle Alexander
"White Rage" Carol Anderson
"Lies my Teacher Told Me" James W. Loewen
"Evicted" Matthew Desmond
"Why are all the Black Kids Sitting Together in the Cafeteria?" Beverly Daniel Tatum
"Malcolm X" Alex Haley (Or the movie with Denzel Washington)
"The Warmth of Other Suns" Isabel Wilkerson
"Between the World and Me" Ta-Nehisi Coates
"Assata" Assata Shakur
"Miseducation of the Negro" Carter G. Woodson
"Eloquent Rage" Brittney Cooper
"The Color of Law" Richard Rothstein (Redlining)
"White Fragility" Robin DiAngelo

"The Color of Money: Black Banks and the Racial Wealth Gap," by Mehrsa Baradaran

"Barracoon: The Story of the Last Black Cargo" Zora Neale Hurston

Colin Kapernick 'Know your Rights Camp'

Jane Elliot - Very blatant & clear cut White woman, Educator on race relations

A couple of brands doing the work:

Calm.com Meditation/Mindfulness Resources

BLM Resources for Change by ThinkLA

Becauseofthemwecan.com

Twitter Suggestions:

@eyesonthestorm

@mikel_jollett

@prisonculture

@nhannahjones & listen to her 1619 Podcast (or read via NY Times)

@TahanieNYC

@telushk

@BreeNewsome

@eveewing

@FredTJoseph

@sonofbaldwin

@ClintSmithIII

@DrIbram & read his book How to be an Anti-Racist

@solomongeorgio

@samswey

Video/Visuals:

Other Authors & Speeches to Listen to: Angela Davis, Audre Lorde, Sonia Sanchez, Nikki Giovanni, Alice Walker, Jamea Baldwin, Bell Hooks, Patricia Hill Collins

Wubr.com Angela Davis

James Baldwin, I am Not your Negro

Watch The Wire, HBO (season 4- more for cultural inner city context)

Black Power Mixtape Movie

Black Panthers: Vanguard of the Revolution, Netflix documentary

Documentary: "Charm City" amazon, pbs 2019

Watchmen, When they See Us, The Banker, American Violet

www.bronzedmoon.com

©

Additional Thank You to my support system for always encouraging me.

Dad, Mom, Sean, Mandy, Letta, Mimi, Hay, Jessica, Markia, Mayra, Bruce & Jazmin.

www.ingramcontent.com/pod-product-compliance
Lightning Source LLC
La Vergne TN
LVHW061257060426
835508LV00015B/1403